The Truth Is in the Pebbles

The Truth Is in the Pebbles

Kristin Brigham

The Truth Is in the Pebbles
       Exploration, Family, and Christian Science
Kristin Brigham
The Truth Is in the Pebbles
By: Kristin Brigham
Copyright 2024
* * * * * * * * * * * * * * *

The author has made every effort possible to ensure the accuracy of the information presented in this book. However, the information herein is sold without warranty, either expressed or implied. Neither the author, publisher, nor any dealer or distributor of this book will be held liable for any damages caused either directly or indirectly by the instructions or information contained in this book. You are encouraged to seek professional advice before taking any action mentioned herein.
* * * * * * * * * * * * * * *

This work depicts actual events in the life of the author as truthfully as recollection permits and/or can be verified by research. Occasionally, dialogue consistent with the character or nature of the person speaking has been augmented or supplemented. The names of some individuals have been changed to respect their privacy. I acknowledge that this is my recollections of the events. Others may recount them differently.
* * * * * * * * * * * * * * *

In accordance with the U.S. Copyright Act of 1976, the scanning, uploading, and electronic sharing of any part of this book without the permission of the publisher is unlawful piracy and theft of the author's intellectual property. If you would like to use material from this book (other than for review purposes), prior written permission can be obtained by contacting the author. Thank you for your support of the author's rights.

* * * * * * * * * * * * * * *

Notice of Rights: All rights reserved. No part of this book may be reproduced or transmitted in any form by any means, electronic, mechanical, photocopy, recording, or other without the prior and express written permission of the author with the exception of brief cited quotes. Thank you for respecting the property rights of this and all authors.

* * * * * * * * * * * * * * *

Permission: For information on getting permission for reprints and excerpts, contact: charles@1mind.io

CONTENTS

1. INTRODUCTION
2. THE FIRST HOUSE
3. WHAT CAME BEFORE
4. OF SCIENTIFIC TRUTH
5. LIFE IN SYRACUSE
6. WEALTH'S HIGHS & LOWS
7. BRINGING UP BABY
8. DEATH KNOCKS
9. COLLEGE FEMINITY
10. LADY LIBERATION
11. FOR LOVE
12. SAIL ON
13. BACK TO SCHOOL
14. CAREER CALLS
15. THE CHRONICLES OF TEENAGERS
16. DISCRIMINATION'S INTERLUDE
17. COAST TO COAST
18. INTROSPECTION
19. WHERE I AM

20. **PATH OF FAITH**
21. **THE NEXT GENERATION**
22. **CONCLUSION**

FORWARD
By Charles Brigham

At six, maybe seven, the earliest recollection of my typical playtime consisted of me running around my childhood home with the backyard stylings of my mother playing the saxophone with decent talent. This type of entertainment was to be predicted in the Brigham household – she always liked to set a fun backdrop for us.

We grew up in the San Francisco Bay Area in the mid-80s. By age nine, my brother and I were trained to explore the Northern West Coast shores. Skilled Marine Biologists, with certificates earned by the Kristin Brigham's University of Exploration and Inquiry. At that time the beaches were next to empty, which left the shore vast and pristine. My mother's voice calling out against the backdrop of the waves to "look over here!" or enticing us to search some other crevice, after already doing so for the last two hours, will be forever engrained into my thoughts. That's how I always remember her in my youth: searching, exploring, crouching, laughing, playing.

The garden around our home in Hayward, California set the stage for my brother and I's first job. We assisted my mother with half an acre of land by pulling weeds and planting seeds. She taught us about plants and flowers and the beauty and fruit they produced. Bright orange California Poppies, chewy licorice and honeysuckle plants, and large pear and plum trees set the perimeter of our house. My mom would make pies from the leftover plums we didn't stuff ourselves with and serve them with freshly whipped cream.

With these memories, all the moments within nature and beauty, she taught us that curating your environment aided in organizing both your external and internal worlds. My appreciation for the relationship one builds and sustains with nature, considering its fickle and selfish demeanor, grew as I observed my mother's poise in her interactions. She gracefully guided the earth to refine her body and sharpen her mind. Even her soul.

Perhaps she carried such calmness due to her avid belief that one does not live only through mind or body, but rather a shared collective of consciousness. This One Mind and all its attributes were truth to her. Life and Love established in all of us allowing infinite ability to discover and evolve with the planet and universe. She demonstrated that we must stay in the action of Love, be active. She imprinted on me that Love is omnipresent, omnipotent and that we are citizens of a Spirit making our way through this earth. She denied any aping of the Divine Mind and exposed it as unreal. She emphasized the need for less "I and you", and more "we and us" as you navigate the roadmap to spiritual destination.

The constant reminisces of my mother I admire in every memory she painted is her demand to view everything through Wisdom. This simple point of view is the lifelong foundation, the minimum. Let that bedrock manifest through any decision thereafter. She taught me that we all must contemplate silently the fruits of our bedrock and constantly work to move away from mental malpractice and more toward faith and spirituality. Through this action we would see the fullness of another person and their contribution to the world and collective consciousness.

She taught that people are more than what we can understand with our material senses. And to break through this terrestrial barrier we must take action in our own spiritual growth. Every step towards goodness is a tendency towards Spirituality. It isn't always easy but it can be easier, and exciting!

I hope that this book inspires others to do amazing things and provides some tools to help when challenged or when presented with opportunities.

Finally, it is my mother's tenacity to better herself, take a constructive approach to challenges, and enjoy opportunities so thoroughly that makes her revered so profoundly by her friends, family, and colleagues.

Her life, as you'll soon find, was filled with rich experiences and significant life lessons. Such as raising two biracial boys alone during one of America's many peak racially aggressive decades while simultaneously earning degrees in Engineering at prestigious schools, which required hours of critical research and work-study. To be one of the only women at the time to advance in Stanford engineering, earning patents along the way. Eventually, watching her two young boys, who admittedly did not always make her juggling act as a single mother, engineer, teacher, an easy one, bring several beautiful grandchildren into this world. Without any surprise, she excelled with flying colors as a supportive, loving, and ever-inquisitive grandmother. Kristin Brigham is nothing less than a mentor to many all over the world.

Everyone has an adventurous story to tell and everyone can learn from each other's stories. People with profound unique experiences like my mother's can assist in amplifying new ideas and experiences. The example of her life enlightened me to believe that we are one consciousness, one mind, and one beautiful story with ever-woven threads that, if brought together, can show us new, unique ways to advance humanity and the world forward.

Born and raised a New Yorker, she lived in NYC during a Renaissance era, defied and challenged the norm. Explored and pioneered physically and mentally through sports and education. Always dynamic. An Alfred, Stanford and Berkley educated woman who has overcome the challenges of being one of the first in her fields of education and engineering. One of the first single white mothers to raise "black" kids to be successful in varying challenging discriminatory environments.

Her mark on the world is yet to be smudged. Her flame still lit. A legacy that will leave all who read her story with inspiration and enlightenment to explore.

DEDICATION & ACKNOWLEDGEMENTS

To my devoted sons, wiggly grandchildren, and those in my life I have had the pleasure to giggle endlessly with, dramatically weep beside, and joined to stuff my face with earth's mouth-watering delicacies.

A thank you to my parents. Without whom, I would have discovered persistent curiosity and determination for truth-seeking much too late in life.

To the people who've been by my side, especially in recent years' heartbreak and wonder. You are my light.

Finally, to the men I've had the honor to call lovers and partners. You've offered a pragmatic girl unforgettable rebellion.

What possibilities will the next life hold?

The Lord is my shepherd; I shall not want.
He maketh me to lie down in green pastures: he leadeth me beside the still waters.
He restoreth my soul: he leadeth me in the paths of righteousness for his name's sake.
Yea, though I walk through the valley of the shadow of death, I will fear no evil: for thou art with me; thy rod and thy staff they comfort me.
Thou preparest a table before me in the presence of mine enemies: thou anointest my head with oil; my Cup runneth over.
Surely goodness and mercy shall follow me all the days of my life: and I will dwell in the house of the Lord for ever.
Psalms 23

I.
INTRODUCTION

A darkening sky and the threat of rain filled me with an all-consuming joy even in my early years. It wasn't the rain I loved but what came after the storm.

The corner of the roof of the first house was home to a peculiar phenomenon that was only released by rain. A rather large amount of grit gathered over time in the corner of the roof — dirt, leaves, twigs, and anything else the wind could lift into the sky before plopping onto the house. One of my first scientific inquiries sat below this heaping pile of sky gunk.

Beneath that corner sat an enchanting little nook, graced by a congregation of barberry bushes resting over gravel and pebbles that decorated the landscape. The bushes were inviting enough by themselves. Their crimson berries glistened like rubies, tempting young fingers to reach out for a taste of its curious mixture of tart and sweet. However, the vibrant pebbles, made new by the rain's wash, revealed a mesmerizing array of shapes, colors, and textures, drawing me to that little corner from one rainstorm to the next for years.

When the rain poured heavily enough, the deluge of water was sufficient to loosen the grit that collected above. With a sudden burst, the heavy stream would not only clear the pipes, but pour out currents that washed everything below. With all the debris blasted away, my special little corner of the world was new again, sparkling pure and refreshed beneath the midday sun.

The moment the rain stopped, I'd rush to that spot where the barberry bushes met the gravel to examine the shiny pebbles. From the age of three years old, I could report on what had changed from the storm before and which rocks had been polished just a bit shinier.

Sitting there, breathing air fragranced by the garden of flowers my mother recently planted, the smell of pavement after being met with rain, and the earthy scent of dirt rising from the ground, I believed I was in a magical place where time stood still. It was my special place and where I longed to be.

This memory being one of my first, perfectly predicts what drives me. Beauty, curiosity, joy. The first house, filled with members who fostered the belief to seek truth, inspired a childhood so rich with life and love, the roadmap for my life was clear. I want to be someone who fosters such curiosity. Encourages rebellious truth seekers. Share joyous love with those who lead with their heart as well. Hence, writing a book filled with my greatest life lessons.

The last two or three months of writing this book have held big challenges for me, including some very cruel treatment during a hospital stay which resulted in a gross degradation of my stamina. Going through these difficulties made me think more deeply about what a memoir is and for whom it is written.

True, chronicling the story of one's life can be merely a personal pursuit where one leaves behind their version of the tales they've spun on earth. For others, however, the desire to write a memoir is borne out of a need to shed light on a particular virtue or value (or set of values) to help others and to enrich the lives of those who read – whether family, friend, or stranger.

For me, the primary driver is to share history. History is lost on a modern generation that tends to think primarily in the future tense. Innovation, change, and improvement are at the heart of this fast-changing culture. Our connection to the present is inextricably tied to the past. The lessons forged there form the foundation we stand on today.

I look to my sons and extended family with hope, joy and confidence about the marks they will make on the world. Therefore, I feel duty-bound to equip them with the faces, places, and events upon which their lives are built.

I am eternally grateful to have been raised to reject limitations and reach for my higher purpose and goal. I was taught the power of integrity and instructed by my parents to value hard work — both physical and mental — and to enjoy the fruits of my labor. In addition, I was gifted a sense of humor, crafted in times of fun and games and tenacity, forged in times of trial and disappointment. These are the treasured concepts I learned as a child.

Additionally, I wish my parents had taken the time to write and share more of their thoughts and insights. I wish I knew more of the details of their journey — their thoughts and emotions about those thoughts. I am thankful for all I remember, but the richness of their lives defies any mere human's ability to remember it all. If only it had all been written down... So that is what I do now for them, for myself, my Charles and Stephan, and for those who follow.

I hope that by writing this memoir, I inspire others to value their own histories, seek out the lessons of the past, and enjoy the satisfaction of offering the world their knowledge and wisdom. Doing so can add joy in times of peace and prosperity and courage in times of trial and suffering.

Being old is such a foreign concept. I feel it only in my body. That said, those childhood days are far behind me. Whether that barberry bush and those shiny pebbles are gracing that little corner, I know not.

It's been nearly 70 years since I stood on that hallowed ground. The person I became because of that sweet spot made my life what it was, is, and will be.

My age, my memories, and the experiences of others in my generation hopefully can be of use in the face of this new world; which I argue is more difficult than the one we faced seven decades ago. True, our threats were bombs, bullets, and body bags. Modern society faces threats grimmer and by far more deceptive. Perhaps the wisdom of their forebearers might serve as a guiding light.

At this time in my life, sailing, skiing, partying, and such are no longer important nor possible for me. However, all life has great meaning and purpose — old and young. That is why I share my story. I hope to be a source of hope, steering all toward love and light.

And we know that in all things God works for the good of those who love him, who[a] have been called according to his purpose.
Romans 8:28

I.
THE FIRST HOUSE

My mother was born in a five-story Queen Anne house. An incredible house. Built anywhere from the 1870s to the 1890s and a symbol for the Reconstruction Era.

The enormous front porch was guarded by a 50ft screened door warding protection from the insects dying to nibble on warm arms and legs. An area beloved for tiny toddlers trotting on tricycles. The porch was right next to the torrent, an imaginative playground for a child to wander safely and locked in, off the streets.

Upon entering, the house bombarded its visitors with curved windows, partnering with soaring wooden pocket doors - insisting you notice the split living room that was divided into a library full of first edition treasures and original manuscripts my grandmother collected. I spent many hours in there losing myself to the adventures of every hero and heroine in their pages. At one time, she owned first editions belonging to Mark Twain, Shakespeare, and other great authors. Of course, these were lost later in the transitions of the market crash.

To the right of the living space was the dining room with pocket doors that closed and curtains for formal dinners every night. The dining room overlooked the lot of land that my grandparents gardened, open for play as well. Behind that was the kitchen. A place I originally called the "shiny room" as it was designed with state-of-the-art finishes and the best appliances of the time. A full basement for storage, pantry goods. Jam, pickles, other fermented goods we made ourselves. Many were the day I joined my mother and grandmother in cooking these jams, learning how to properly ferment foods, and creating delectable feasts. With hands stained purple and the sweet taste of jelly on our tongues, we moved dozens upon dozens of bottles into the pantry — our insurance against any ills to come.

The house pined for walks down the long hallways that stretched from the front of the house to the back. Each floor above the main was less ornate, but just as spacious. The second floor held the master bedroom for my grandparents, their bathroom which was in a separate room, which for those times in America was a fascinating blueprint for a home. Two other bedrooms filled that floor. The third floor had three more bedrooms, and the attic, or top of the torrent, was a typical area for dust and streams of light from the roof.

A host of pets shared the grounds with us. Long Island was a country region at the time, unspoiled by modernization, development, and change. Farms dotted the wide-open landscape of fields that beckoned a curious child like me to run until my legs turned to jelly. This also meant we'd pick up a stray barn animal here and there. My family never turned them away and they'd often become akin to pets for us.

A favorite of mine was a goat who wandered into our garden and never left. To this day, I'm not sure where he came from, we never bothered asking him. Once he arrived and decided our land was his new home, he was inseparable from our family. He loved head scratches and once you fulfilled his request he was stuck to you like glue. An unexpectedly affectionate little creature and never once wandered from our home nor our little ragtag group during our family excursions. As a child, this was a wonderful and easy addition to the family. My parents equally accepted him as one of their own. I hadn't appreciated the carefree nature of my mother and father until I was older – it seemed like common sense to sit in the backseat beside my friend goat at the time. They never batted an eye as we loaded up the car, complete with five children, one boxer, and a goat who refused to be left behind.

Along with the animals, a pack of humans also lived in the first house. Occupants consisted of me, my three uncles, three aunts, my mother, my mother's mother, Lydia Mary Owen, and my grandfather, Peter G Schilling.

I knew my maternal Grandmother as FiFi. The first sight that comes to mind when I imagine her in the house is the twinkle in her eye. She was the beating heart that gave life to the house. Her mother died in childbirth. Her father was Roger Williams Peese, who was one of general Grant's chief surgeons for a period of time but had to return home three times to heal himself from injuries during war.

He'd come home and share a few stories about the war and Fifi would listen intently as she was never asked to leave during such "violent discussions." Her family was known for the intellect of their women, and they lived much more to how women live today. Though abnormal for women of her time, she was encouraged by her father to adopt an independent mind.

Peese was also a philanthropist, responsible for establishing a hospital in the White House. This, among the multiple hospitals he co-founded, remained his passion until the end of his life, establishing St. Joseph's Hospital in New York. After the war ended, my great-grandfather was a surgeon in Syracuse. An assistant cut him during an operation, which led to an infection. He died shortly after.

As an orphan, FiFi inherited everything, making her perhaps the only wealthy free-thinking single woman of her time. She was taken in and raised by her aunt Elsie who never married but was a world traveler and sold jewelry to prominent wealth. Elsie further sculpted Fifi's independence and empowerment.

FiFi decided to travel Europe with Elsie after graduating from Syracuse University, the top of her class. She made good friends with the founders of one of the first ceramics museums in New York, and was active in social political discussions, taking an interest in international social structures when she landed in Germany.

By age 26, she was "on the shelf" which is another century's way of saying she was too old to marry. Petite, wiry, brownish skin (not a peaches and cream complexion like her family) very brainy, witty, and obviously unlike most women around her. She enjoyed the opera, museums, eating foreign foods - a woman of modern times. Truth be told, she was exceptionally ordinary for the 21st century; but an absolute trailblazer of the times at hand.

My grandfather, a Norwegian man happily living anywhere other than Norway, finished his physics degree in Germany. He came from one of the wealthiest families in Norway — who impressed on him the importance of education and exploration rather than gallivanting and spending his inheritance like other boys in his circle had done. He was lanky, blue eyes, blonde hair, and very good looking.

As the story goes, when he met Fifi during a visit to Germany, Papa's breath was taken away. The pair fell in love quickly and genuinely enjoyed each other's company. I emphasize *genuinely* because couples at that time married often for reasons other than love. Even the ones who did marry for love did not always seem to enjoy each other's company. Perhaps I was too young to make such assumptions, although I still believe couples today struggle to genuinely enjoy those they claim to love. Perhaps I'm too old to make such assumptions now. According to Fifi's account of events, they could talk about anything, which was refreshing and new for her. Eventually, she convinced Papa to come to America. It wasn't a hard sell since he loved the United States and what it stood for in its best attempts.

Oh how they enjoyed each other so much! Their love affair led to their immediate marriage which led to the conception of my mother. As I remember, Papa always had a strong accent. My mother would often mimic it in the comedic or overly dramatic retelling of stories about her youth. He and Fifi spoke German to each other when they didn't want the children to understand them. Occasionally, amongst nosey neighbors as well.

Papa adored the sea as do nearly all Norwegians. It wasn't uncommon for our family to spend the entire day in the ocean. We were in the water so often, we joked that we had gills for lungs. Our Norwegian heritage sparked our double life — one on land and one in the water. I suppose this is why I was so drawn to the sea all these years. Something I hadn't realized until recollecting on my grandparents.

Papa was a loving man though stern about some things. He was quite particular about what we ate, believing food to be the elixir of life.

Being from Europe, he had to adjust to America's taste in meat. He'd often return home from the butcher, greet the family in the backyard, and say to Fifi; "You know, you just can't find grilled pork the way you like it in the US. – Fatty and crusty."

Somehow, they learned to make do together. They loved cooking beside one another. The meals Fifi crafted were so magical. In the evenings, still in earshot of the waves, dinner would be served in fashion. Everyone dressed up, every night, as if entertaining elite guests (more times than not, there would be a few). My parents would join my grandparents in preparing the meals, although Papa and Fifi were clearly the head chefs. Dressed and pressed, us children of our family played games to pass the time until the gameplay grew too rough. It often did. Then some adult put us out by gently warning us not to ruin our nice clothes.

When the dinner bell sounded, we assembled in our usual spots in the dining room as Papa marched in with a platter of delicious meat he and Fifi cooked. The aromas wafting from the kitchen intensified as the dishes made their way into the dining area still sizzling or bubbling fresh from the stove.

Thankfully, the kids had their own table where we'd sit and chow down unmannerly until scolded to behave. Meanwhile, at the grand table, the grown-ups laughed, talked politics, and debated all the important issues of the world.

These were my memories of the first house, a place that breathed life, dance, giggles, creation, lust, love and tears. The history of the people who stayed here glued the paper to the walls. My Fifi and Papa poured themselves into this gigantic home and their story echoed down every hallway, cupboard and staircase. What was produced from this incubator of grit and spirit was generations of love in abundance. I was blessed to begin my story here, with these people. Only now do I feel their warmth again as I grow closer to seeing them again.

How good and pleasant it is
*   when God's people live together in unity!*
It is like precious oil poured on the head,
running down on the beard,
running down on Aaron's beard,
down on the collar of his robe.
It is as if the dew of Hermon
were falling on Mount Zion.
For there the Lord bestows his blessing,
even life forevermore.
Psalm 133: 1-3

II.
WHAT CAME BEFORE

My father's childhood home was a road away from the big house where my mother and the rest of us eventually lived. My parents grew up just two miles away from each other in Syracuse, NY although they didn't meet until they attended the same high school in Long Island.

My mother could only be accurately described as the epitome of vitality. She was a competitive swimmer in her youth and, like my father, had looks that could kill. She stood at 5'7", which, at that time was akin to a giant for a woman. Her charm and intelligence stood even taller as she could outwit anyone in any room.

Upon their first meeting, she took my father's breath away. But it was her winsome personality that prompted him to want to spend his life with her.

Eventually, when time came, Mom took her new beau to meet her parents. They scanned him over and questioned his intentions, highly skeptical that my father was only interested in my mother's looks rather than her brain. They were concerned he'd downplay her intelligence, dull her opportunities, and dominate her, as did other men who couldn't abide a woman with ambition and smarts. They desperately wanted my mother to avoid a life where she was dependent on a man, and feared my mother would be trapped by marriage through the coercion of societal standards.

After countless discussions between my father and grandparents, coupled with Fifi and Papa's observations of my parents' interlude, they were convinced to approve the match. It was clear to anyone who saw my mom and dad together that they were head over heels in love. My grandparents could not reasonably withhold their blessing for the two to marry. My mother, being older than standard to start a family, was thrilled to get the show on the road. Soon after the marriage, their lives were blessed with children, starting with me.

Proving that "into each life some rain must fall," the rumble of war broke out in Europe in 1939. My family prayed the war would not reach into our country and take our young men over the oceans and away from us. To our shock and disappointment, the fight was prolonged. Just two years later, the US joined the war. Before long, young men and their able-bodied fathers and uncles were called to serve.

By 1946, many members of my family and others in our community were sent off to fight in World War II. I, like everyone who had fighting-aged males in their homes, had to learn to live with the absence of the men we loved most. My father and three uncles prepared to say goodbye for what my mother prayed was a short separation.

My family watched as my father drove away, waving goodbye with heavy hearts and tear-stained cheeks. I was far too young to know how long this goodbye would last.

His parents urged him to find a way to return to us as soon as possible. In those days, families with only one son could be exempted from sending their young men to war. But my father wouldn't take the exemption, despite qualifying for it. By choice, he was not to be spared. He considered it his duty to fight for country, flag, and family. He would not stay behind. Nor would my three uncles who were shipped overseas with their brother-in-law to join the fray.

My father served in WWII proudly doing work called, "flying the hump" over the mountains from India to China to support the Chinese war effort against Japan. His main duty was to get airplanes and supplies across the Himalayas, navigating weather that was harsh and unpredictable. There were no satellites in those days and no clear routes to their destinations that were untouched by potential enemy bombs. Every maneuver was a learning experience and every lesson a baptism by fire. If men could somehow manage to stay alive, they were considered expert navigators.

When my father left to serve, stress levels rose on both sides of the family. Just as I was my father's favorite (a secret I've held onto long enough), my father was my grandmother's. Fifi adored her son-in-law. Perhaps it was the way he over-delivered on their expectations as a suitable husband to her only daughter. Sometimes, when I ponder it too much, I think it had to do with her deep gratitude for Papa, and belief no man could compare. Until my father. She saw our future in him.

She could barely manage the emotional toll of watching all four of her sons leave the safety of American shores for Europe. We all knew our shores wouldn't be safe if brave men didn't go.

As a toddler, I lacked a true understanding of it all, but I lived each day with the symptoms of it. Even toddlers were not exempt from carrying some tiny part of the collective burden of the conflict and missing men. I saw the tears. I heard the whispers of women in quiet corners. I saw the weeping children and wives who just received the news their goodbyes to the man of their house were their last. I noticed every day my father wasn't there to pat me on the back or shoo me off to bed at night. The air was thick with despair and anticipation.

My mother, Fifi, and Papa waited on bated breath for news of the boys. This was not the outcome they envisioned when they married and started their family. No one imagined war. How could they?

We were blessed. As families all around us received visits from military officers announcing the passing of their sons, all four men of our family eventually came home without so much as a scratch — at least not physically. The mental wounds, though invisible, were there. And there was no professional discourse in those times to assist the men, the country, to process those wounds. We all either counted our blessings or grieved alone.

Most stories from this time were about how families dealt with the loss. Once, years later, my mother described to me the great survivor's guilt she'd often feel when her brothers and my father returned home. Unlike Fifi, who only sang glee for her family, my mom constantly asked us to tend to families who lost. One family in particular never left her mind.

Fifi and Papa were good friends with the editor of a notable newsprint — one that is still in business today. My mother and her closest friend, Emily, the daughter of the editor, had started a newspaper for fun when they were children, modeling the work Emily's parents did. They'd meet at the beach to draft articles and draw images and comics before distributing the paper to the homes of their community. Mama and Emily were inseparable at that time, as my mother described it. As they got older, they remained extremely close and Emily was just as much of a fan of my father.

Before the war, our family and Emily's were inseparable. We shared many dinners with them then, and during the conflict. She was like an aunt to me. The adults would tease she could marry one of my uncles so they'd all officially be family.

Emily had only one brother who could have claimed his exemption from the war, being the only male to carry the family name into the future. Like my father, he refused his exit, also believing it was his duty to serve. He volunteered for service and proudly left for the violent theatre of conflict. Just a couple weeks after departing, Emily's brother was killed, dying at bloody onslaught of his squad's position. My mother was at Emily's side.

When the men in our family returned home, we saw Emily and her family less and less until they completely ended contact with my mother and, by default, the rest of the family. I missed Emily and learned years later what happened. My mother explained to me that Emily's family suffered immeasurable grief. While they loved our family, they couldn't endure watching Fifi and Papa welcome home one son after another until all four sons returned safely. It was a sting they couldn't bear as the fighting had taken their only heir. Seeing the life within our home only reminded them of the death in theirs.

Upon confronting Emily, my mother said Emily asked her why she was allowed to keep an abundant amount of blessings when others are losing more than any one person can endure. This changed my mother's outlook and after that she volunteered to aid families who lost fathers and providers in the war.

Although I was barely three years old when it happened, I remember my father walking back through the door to the cheers and happy tears of our family members. I could also sense the deep sadness everyone felt day after day as the war continued and friends were injured or killed. People do not often like to talk about this part of war — the daily living of it. The news reports. The fear. The injuries. The deaths.

The war seeped into every conversation. It dominated their waking hours and haunted their silent dreams. The inability to escape it was a burden they bore for years until living with the war was a part of our daily routine, making it challenging even to relish the moments of joy in their lives. Birthdays, anniversaries, graduations, pregnancies, births, and every other joyous occasion was sucked up by the battle a continent away. It poisoned the air. Those who breathed it in more deeply couldn't bear to be around those who chose not to.

My father never discussed the horrors of war with us. He, like other men at that time, developed a stiff upper lip and dealt with the trauma of the horrors they had seen and heard in the capsules of their own minds. Whatever terrors my father and the others had witnessed were buried deep inside — traumas that were never to be shared with my siblings and me.

Fifi, on the other hand, chose gratitude instead of anger to deal with the pain that surrounded her. She was the lifeblood of her home, filling it with energy and love. My grandmother attributed all of her boys' survival to divine science. She believed each of them still had a purpose to fulfill, hence their survival of the hellfires of World War II. I learned she had something of a secret weapon with this.

Do not conform to the pattern of this world, but be transformed by the renewing of your mind. Then you will be able to test and approve what God's will is—his good, pleasing and perfect will.
  Romans 12:2

IV.
OF SCIENTIFIC TRUTH

An author's note as you, reader, venture into this section and forward of my story. I wish not to share my beliefs with the notion one must know it to be truth. In fact, there is a desire in me to withhold such a profession of my stance on religion. That said, there is an equal desire to share only so someone may find some roadmap to their spiritual destination.

Ultimately, my decision to include this in my book is nothing more than to explain the depth in which I live my life by these principles. Due to my heritage, such beliefs may be in my blood. My hope is that one may read and not feel coerced, rather embrace my words as simply another testimony – take it or leave it. I pray everyone simply lives to seek truth and love, here is mine.

My family lineage has roots that are deeply embedded in the Quaker religious tradition. The Quakers, also known as the Religious Society of Friends, was a Christian denomination known for their emphasis on simplicity, equality, peace, integrity, and community.

Started by George Fox and Margaret Fell in 1600's Britain, Quakers believed that God could be found among His people rather than strictly in churches. This was a radical belief at the time as the church was the heart of British government, polity, and life.

To be of Quaker extraction and adhering to its beliefs and practices meant possible persecution at any time. The British church held itself in the highest regard and would not abide anyone who dared to think differently. My ancestors and the rest of the Quakers practiced the most benign expressions of faith: silent worship, consensus decision-making, and testimonies that advocated for social justice and pacifism.

Under threat, my ancestors came to America to escape persecution from British religious attackers. They did so peacefully as they did not bear arms. They were active abolitionists and believed in peace at all costs. Therefore, they had to hire bodyguards for protection who bore arms for them. Though never passive, my forebears were gentle, loving people.

The roots of the Quaker faith in my family stretch back to my great-grandparents' time. My grandmother's grandfather was an active Quaker who played a significant role in the saving young men's lives during the post-Civil War era. Working alongside a dedicated group of nuns, they provided essential medical care to the injured.

During the Civil War, he and his colleagues were deeply involved in tending to wounded soldiers. The scenes he witnessed were harrowing, and he often described the carnage of the war as unimaginably horrific. Faces were twisted and mangled, and limbs were shattered and lost. He vividly recounted the agonizing moments when doctors and nurses, despite their best efforts, had to watch hundreds of men succumb to their injuries at the height of the conflict. The memories of those grim days left an indelible mark on him, shaping his commitment to compassion and care, principles that remain central to the Quaker faith.

My ancestors sailed to the New World in hopes of finding a chance to peacefully worship. Sadly, even in their new American home, Quakers faced persecution and fled once again. In truth, my family was also opposed to organized religion. It was one of the basic tenets of their belief system. For me Christian Science encapsulated this tenant – Church is the structure of Truth and Love; whatever rests upon and proceeds from divine Principle. I found this ironic that a group could be persecuted, given that they too did not wish to create division, even to the point of removing themselves peacefully from the situation and uprooting their lives. Similarly, I learned in my Christian Science practice that Mary Baker Eddy, the founder of Christian Science, had to dissolve the church twice because of suspicions of organized religion. I believe my family mimicked this reaction to conflict, and like Mary Baker Eddy, would continue to find like-minded individuals that shared the belief to spread truth and love.

For my parents, organized religion held little appeal. Perhaps that is why my father and my mother easily embraced the tenets of Christian Science, which was free from the constraints of typical church doctrine, but believed in the power of love and the overall progression of one's mind, body and spirit. In our home, the concept of material matter as a form of thought was foreign- or more poignantly, the idea that *the act of conceptualizing physical matter itself* is actually a form of thought was central to our understanding of reality — a belief that would become the cornerstone of my faith and the bedrock of my spiritual journey.

At about twelve, my mother sat me down and explained the religion and why she chose it. She liked that the services do not have a pastor, readings are shared from the Bible and the Christian Science textbook. Leaders are elected by the members. It all made sense to me and had none of the trappings of wealth, fame, and power that often marred the standard Christian faith.

When I first learned about Christian Science, I was struck by its unique perspective on faith, healing, and life itself. At the heart of my faith is the belief in the power of prayer and the healing presence of truth. This was a radical shift for me, coming from a time in history where medicine and faith were seen as separate entities. Christian Science taught that being critical is key, however love is ever-present and that understanding this truth can lead to physical healing and spiritual growth.

I found that both exciting and intriguing. I was always hungry for more knowledge. I learned that Mary Baker Eddy, the founder of Christian Science, wrote the central text of our faith: Science and Health with Key to the Scriptures. This book, along with the Bible, quickly refined the cornerstone of my belief in Christian Science teachings. I learned that God is good, loving, and all-powerful. Therefore, he was able to bless his children with life and health.

One of the most transformative concepts for me was the idea that our true identity is spiritual, not material. We aren't just flesh and bone. There is something more real about us than our physical bodies: our spirits. This meant that illnesses, injuries, and even sin are seen as misunderstandings of my true spiritual identity. Sin itself is simply missing the mark. This leaves room for interpretation, although the belief that we are anything less than ever-evolving perfect creatures, designed to create mistakes, is false.

Through prayer and a deepening understanding of God's nature, I worked to correct and eliminate these misunderstandings so that I could experience healing.

Prayer did not grow for me from something I did for the purpose of asking God to intervene. Instead, prayer became a vehicle for aligning my thoughts with divine truth.

One of the things I loved most about my faith was the community of Christian Science believers we had surrounding us. We attended services at the church that were simple and focused on readings from the Bible and Science and Health. There was no ordained clergy; instead, members took turns reading and leading the services. This fostered a sense of equality and shared responsibility within the congregation.

I also enjoyed hearing people share their testimonies, short stories from people across the Christian Science community. Wednesday Church service healing testimonies. A testimony could center around just about anything: a healing, a spiritual insight, a personal story of blessing. They all pointed back to Christian Science as the source of their gifts. These testimonies were powerful and often deeply moving because they were people we knew and loved. They were, essentially, living proof of the principles we were learning.

Learning Christian Science was a gradual process. There were moments of revelation and deeper levels of understanding that forced me to undergo a shift in my thinking. At times, I had to adopt the willingness to see the world through a spiritual lens rather than a purely physical one. It wasn't always easy, but it was profoundly rewarding to make that leap to placing the emphasis on understanding and demonstrating God's love in daily life. This brought me a sense of purpose and joy both in childhood and in adulthood.

My relationship with the church was not destined to be eternally positive. There were times when I felt the church was not present for my family. I would have to learn to reconcile what I thought was positive with the other parts that were less than appealing.

My greatest gratitude for my faith and the childhood that fostered it is the room to find your own conclusions. I encourage anyone reading this to find their own beliefs. To be critical of all truths. To seek contradictions until there is no deniable answer before them. Then, sit with that truth in love and joy.

These commandments that I give you today are to be on your hearts. Impress them on your children. Talk about them when you sit at home and when you walk along the road, when you lie down and when you get up.

Deuteronomy 6:6-7

V.

LIFE IN SYRACUSE

Part of our family had settled in western New York, around Skaneateles Lake. Our whole family had been involved in an underground rescue operation in Syracuse, helping people escape religious persecution, a legacy of service that ran deep in our family's history.

During this time, my mother announced she was pregnant with another child. I watched with fascination as her belly grew larger and larger, month by month, until it was finally time for her to deliver. The anticipation filled our household, and I found myself constantly wondering about this new sibling who would soon join our family.

My father worked as an airplane mechanic for Pan American Airways, a position that carried enormous responsibility. Every day, he diligently ensured their planes wouldn't fall from the sky, drawing on the same careful attention to detail he had developed during the war. His work demanded precision, people's lives literally depended on his expertise and thoroughness. However, Papa, with his characteristic wisdom and foresight, encouraged my father to pursue a college degree to ensure long-term stability for our growing family.

The path to higher education hadn't been available to my father in his youth. My paternal grandfather had died when my father was only fourteen, forcing him to leave school and start working immediately to support his family. Without this tragic interruption, he would have gone directly to college after high school graduation. The lost opportunity had always weighed on him, making Papa's encouragement all the more meaningful.

Despite these early hardships, my father remained strongly in favor of returning to school. His parents had raised him in Douglas Manor, a prestigious neighborhood in Queens, though they had lived in the smallest house in the community, a humbling reminder that appearances don't always reflect reality. This experience taught him valuable lessons about finding dignity and purpose regardless of material circumstances.

My father was exceptionally well-read, thanks largely to his own father, who had worked as a publisher. Their modest home had been filled with books of every description, and my father had quickly fallen in love with reading and the power that came from educating himself. Books became his window to a larger world, feeding an intellectual curiosity that would last his entire lifetime.

What truly set my father apart was his remarkable ability to build or fix anything, from automobiles to farm equipment. He never needed to visit a mechanic because he simply had an intuitive mind for understanding how things worked. This natural mechanical aptitude, combined with his love of learning, made engineering the perfect field for him. He enrolled at Syracuse University as an Engineering major, the same institution I would later call my alma mater.

I was fortunate to visit my father during his graduate school years, and those visits left an indelible impression on me. My eyes widened at the sight of the impressive array of laboratory equipment spread throughout the engineering building. Something about that environment, the gleaming instruments, the sense of discovery and possibility, sparked something deep within me that would follow me into my own studies and career. I could see that the love of science was truly passed down from generation to generation in our family. Even though it found different expressions in different people, we were all enamored with the STEM fields.

With another baby on the way and the pressures of graduate school mounting, my father felt urgency to finish his degree as quickly as possible and secure a higher-paying position. The timing created an almost impossible situation. On the day my mother went into labor with Ralph, my father was sitting in class, preparing to take his crucial physics final examination. When word reached him that the baby was coming, he faced a heart-wrenching decision. Without hesitation, he left the exam halfway through, jumped on his motorcycle, and raced twenty miles through city streets to the hospital, determined to be present for the birth of his son.

After finishing college, my father secured an excellent position in Syracuse. This was during a remarkable period in American history when the country had developed its own robust centers of industry, with manufacturing plants being built across the nation. Rather than importing goods from other countries as we do today, American factories provided goods to American consumers. Few places were as industrially active as New York and the New England region, which formed the hub of American manufacturing at that time.

When my father completed his degree, he made a decision that would transform our entire lifestyle. He moved our family to fifteen acres of beautiful farmland in the Syracuse countryside. This new property offered us something precious: the ability to grow our own food on an expansive plot of land. In those days, it was commonplace for families to maintain large gardens, growing peppers, corn, tomatoes, and storing enough potatoes and onions to sustain the family through the harsh North Atlantic winters.

I loved this new property almost as much as our first house. From my earliest days, I had naturally followed in my father's footsteps, both figuratively and literally. I would trudge behind him as he walked into the woods to explore and gather food, absorbing every lesson he shared. He patiently taught me about flowers and plants, which ones could be safely eaten and which ones to avoid at all costs. We did some hunting together, and he showed me how to move silently through the forest, approaching the small game that called our property home without disturbing the natural quiet of the woods.

What I found curious, even then, was that my brothers weren't particularly interested in these outdoor activities most of the time. This meant I often got to be alone with my father, creating precious one-on-one time as he taught me to shoot a rifle or handle a bow and arrow. I learned to use hunting-style bows with steel-tipped arrows, and from a remarkably young age, I accompanied my father to target practice sessions where I learned to shoot .22 rifles, 12-gauge shotguns, and 16-gauge rifles. We would bring clay skeets and launch them into the air, and I would track them and shoot them down, my tiny hands confidently wrapped around firearms that seemed almost too large for my small frame.

Of course, my father understood that knowing how to safely handle weapons when they weren't in use was just as critical as learning to use them effectively. He was strict about the importance of properly locking up all weapons after every hunting trip or practice session. He firmly believed that any educated, responsible person could, and should, learn how to handle firearms safely, but this knowledge came with serious responsibilities that were never to be taken lightly.

My father was fundamentally a simple man who had grown up without the considerable wealth that my mother's family had enjoyed for generations. He had learned early in life to work skillfully with his hands, both as an engineer and as a mechanic. These weren't just jobs for him, they were expressions of his character and his approach to solving problems in the world.

He was quite simply the smartest person I knew, and the smartest person most people in our community knew as well. When he took a standardized aptitude test, he scored in the remarkable 99th percentile, placing him among the most intellectually gifted individuals in the general population. Years later, when I took that same test, I scored in the 97th percentile, a result that filled us both with pride and suggested clearly that intellectual ability was among the many precious gifts he had passed down to me.

Intelligence wasn't the only thing I inherited from my father. We shared a deep, abiding love of science fiction that continues to enrich my life today. We would spend countless hours discussing the books we'd read, exploring the imaginative worlds that talented writers had created. While I continue to read science fiction voraciously, I find myself avoiding the darker, more cruel varieties that seem popular today. Instead, I gravitate toward stories that combine excellent writing with strong, positive imagination, tales that inspire rather than merely frighten.

We worked our bodies as diligently as we worked our minds. Every year brought new hockey sticks and pucks, and our household, like most in our region, would strap on skis whenever a nor'easter blessed our fields with heavy snow. A good snowfall was always the perfect excuse to abandon regular chores and schoolwork to go skiing through our neighborhood and the surrounding countryside. We also had well-made sleds that were remarkably easy to steer, allowing us to navigate the hills and valleys of our property with both speed and control.

One particularly memorable summer, my father rented a cottage on Long Island Sound. There were only about a dozen cottages in that remote location, creating an intimate, peaceful community. Those weeks were absolutely heaven on earth for our family. We spent our days simply playing and eating, without schedules or obligations beyond enjoying each other's company and the natural beauty surrounding us. I honestly don't think I was ever happier at any other time in my entire life.

Looking back, I realize we did many things that would be considered dangerous by today's safety-conscious standards. We explored dense forests without constant adult supervision, dove into water of unknown depths, and climbed high up rocky outcroppings and tall trees. But this freedom from excessive restrictions allowed our souls to soar in ways that shaped our confidence and independence. That profound feeling of freedom and possibility stayed with me throughout all the days of my life, influencing how I approached challenges and opportunities long into adulthood.

In 1949, when I was five or six years old, my parents borrowed enough money from my grandparents to purchase a new house that would become our permanent family home. After this move, I could no longer walk to school as I had before. Instead, I joined the daily ritual of standing outside every morning, waiting for the school bus to arrive. But on special days, my father would surprise me by putting me on the back of his motorcycle and personally driving me to school, those rides were thrilling adventures that made ordinary school days feel magical and special.

Even now, many years later, I sometimes find myself driving past the houses where my parents spent their youth. Both structures are still standing today, weathered by time but fundamentally sound, serving as physical reminders of the foundation that shaped everything that followed in my life.

Let your conversation be without covetousness; and be content with such things as ye have: for he hath said, I will never leave thee, nor forsake thee.

    Hebrews 13:5

VI.
WEALTH'S HIGHS & LOWS

The state of my family's wealth in the early 1920s was sufficient to last many generations. Both sides of the family, but especially my father's side, had carefully amassed substantial real estate holdings and diverse investments that should have been passed down to their children's children for generations to come. However, fate and the devastating economic forces of the late 1920s would determine otherwise.

The stock market crash of 1929 remains one of the most catastrophic financial events in United States history, fundamentally altering the economic landscape of the nation and destroying fortunes that had taken generations to build. No family of means was spared from its destructive reach. Prior to the crash, the US stock market had been experiencing an unprecedented and historic bull run throughout the 1920s, with stock prices rising continuously and seemingly without limit. This sustained period of speculation saw millions of people invest their savings or borrow money to buy stocks, pushing prices to unsustainable levels, creating a dangerous stock market bubble that would inevitably burst with devastating consequences.

Many investors engaged heavily in margin buying, which meant they stood to lose enormous sums of money if the market turned down or even if it failed to advance quickly enough. This practice of purchasing stocks with borrowed money became alarmingly widespread, creating a house of cards that seemed stable only as long as prices continued their upward trajectory. The speculative fervor reached such heights that rational economic principles were abandoned in favor of blind optimism and the belief that stock prices could only go up.

Even a century later, economists and historians continue to debate the multiple interconnected factors that caused this financial catastrophe. Equally relevant issues included overpriced shares, public panic, rising bank loans, an agriculture crisis, higher interest rates, and a cynical press that added to the growing disarray. The crash was caused by many factors including the economic boom following World War I, overproduction in key industries, increased use of margin for purchasing stocks, and lack of global buyers around the world due to the war's aftermath. However, on Black Monday, October 28, 1929, the Dow Jones Industrial Average declined nearly 13 percent, and the ultimate trigger was a complete loss of confidence in the US market that spread like wildfire through investor communities.

For my relatives, as for countless other American families, the stock market crash marked the beginning of the end of our comfortable and seemingly secure financial legacy. The crash swept all of my grandparents' carefully accumulated wealth down the drain along with the fortunes of millions of other investors across the nation. Many investors and ordinary people lost their entire savings, while numerous banks and companies went bankrupt. Thankfully, Papa was not the sort of man to succumb to panic or resort to the desperate measures that some investors took during those dark days, including the tragic suicides that became symbolic of the crash's human toll.

Though many people throughout the country felt that the Great Depression was some kind of divine punishment or cosmic curse visited upon America, my grandparents never embraced such a fatalistic or bitter perspective. They refused to believe they were being punished for some unknown transgression. Much like her attitude toward being blessed with four sons and a husband who returned home safely from the war, Fifi had taught our family to remain grateful for what she called the scientific divine design of life. In her deeply held philosophical view, nothing happened that wasn't meant to be, and even devastating setbacks served some greater purpose that might not be immediately apparent but would eventually reveal its wisdom.

Despite their remarkably positive mindset and philosophical acceptance of their changed circumstances, my grandparents did, however, face the harsh practical reality of their situation. They were forced to part with some of Papa's most favorite and treasured possessions, selling precious items that held deep sentimental value in order to cover essential household bills and care for the family's day-to-day needs. Each sale represented not just a financial transaction, but an emotional sacrifice that chipped away at the material reminders of better times.

My mother would often describe with particular fondness one of the magnificent cars they had owned when she was a child, during the prosperous years before the crash. She said it was an exceptionally fine automobile, luxuriously appointed and covered entirely in the finest leather. It was, in fact, a prestigious Packard, a brand that Papa had especially loved for its combination of engineering excellence and elegant styling. During those affluent years, he had employed professional chauffeurs to drive his family around the city and surrounding areas, allowing himself and his family to indulge freely in the many luxuries that substantial wealth could provide. All of these extravagant possessions and lifestyle choices, including the magnificent ancestral home that had sheltered multiple generations of our family, were eventually lost to the relentless economic pressures of the Great Depression.

As a direct result of the 1929 crash and the widespread financial devastation that followed, the United States government was compelled to institute comprehensive new regulations designed to prevent future catastrophic market crashes and provide better protection for individual investors. However, families like ours would have to completely rebuild their wealth from the ground up before they could benefit from these new protective measures. My grandfather approached this daunting challenge with characteristic determination and practical wisdom, working tirelessly to rebuild his estate while simultaneously teaching his sons the essential skills and principles they would need to do the same for their own families.

Living together in the family home became one of the most effective strategies for keeping expenses manageable while the family focused their energy and resources on the slow, difficult process of financial recovery. This arrangement provided both economic efficiency and emotional support during an extremely challenging period. After my father returned home from the war for good, however, he and my mother made the difficult but necessary decision to leave the comfort and security of living in the big house with my grandparents and strike out on their own to build an independent life.

I genuinely hated the prospect of moving away from that beloved family home. The house itself held so many precious memories, and the neighborhood had become my entire world. However, I had to admit that the surrounding area was populated with more than enough children to provide constant companionship and entertainment. It had become a community much beloved by parents who could be seen daily walking alongside children learning to ride bicycles, dotting the tree-lined streets beside kids who threw balls back and forth and jumped rope with endless energy and enthusiasm. I was the only girl in this particular neighborhood and had been forced to learn to be tough and resilient, adapting my play style to compete and cooperate with boys as my mother continued giving birth to one boy after another. Just as I had finally gotten all the complex social dynamics figured out and felt truly comfortable in my role, it was time to pull up stakes once again and face the challenge of making new friends in an entirely new place.

Despite the sadness of leaving, I had genuinely loved my life in that first house we called home after leaving my grandparents' estate. I can still remember the most special times there as vividly as if they had occurred just yesterday, each memory preserved with crystal clarity in my mind. The greatest gift of that period was being surrounded constantly by extended family, a treasure whose true value was far more precious than my young mind could possibly conceive or appreciate at the time. Still, I understood even then that it was time for my parents to make their own independent way in the world, to establish their own household and create their own family traditions. So our little nuclear family moved into another home, this one surrounded by expansive acres of beautiful land much like the property that Fifi and Papa had once enjoyed during their most prosperous years.

My parents were strongly and philosophically opposed to the idea of living in the conventional upper-middle-class suburban neighborhoods that were becoming increasingly popular in post-war America. My mother, in particular, found these developments far too stuffy, restrictive, and ultimately boring for her tastes and values. Instead, they wanted substantial land that they could build upon according to their own vision, plant with life according to their own preferences, and watch as their children enjoyed the freedom to roam and explore the earth without excessive influence or interference from the outside world. They believed deeply that children needed space to grow, both physically and emotionally, and that connection to the natural world was essential for proper development and character formation.

For a just man falleth seven times, and riseth up again: but the wicked shall fall into mischief.

Rejoice not when thine enemy falleth, and let not thine heart be glad when he stumbleth:

Lest the LORD see it, and it displease him, and he turn away his wrath from him.

Fret not thyself because of evil men, neither be thou envious at the wicked; 20 For there shall be no reward to the evil man; the candle of the wicked shall be put out.

Proverbs 24:16-19

VII.

Bringing Up Baby

My parents had quite an unusual but effective parenting style. They treated us like little animals, letting us out in the morning like chickens being freed from the coop. My brothers played while I roamed in the woods, planting seeds, uprooting weeds, and searching for crawling creatures to perform less than ethical experiments on.

The house was filled with several mouths to feed; often, we were directed to go out on our own adventures to find food — not so much because we needed it as we needed to learn the skill. In truth, food was abundant on our estate. Nearly everything we ate came from our garden.

Though my parents were a team, they had vastly different roles when it came to us children. My father chose apathy as his main tactic of child-rearing, choosing to defer to my mother for the primary parenting responsibilities. By designating my mother as the main communicator to the children, he aggregated his responsibility to get active and involved. As a result, I viewed his strained relationships with both my brothers as his fault. In a way, he suffered the loss of the closeness he craved with his sons.

My brother, Michael, was sent off to military school. Before he left, my father insisted that he cut his hair. It was the main topic of conversation in our home for an entire week. To my parents' detriment, they condoned lively debate, as long as it was respectful, from us children to our mother. If there were an argument my father had with one of us, she would be the one to ease my father's swift ruling so we could draw out our arguments. Nonetheless, if my father was adamant about something, say, cutting my brother's hair so he arrives at military school a step in his favor, my father would win.

Michael was sure he had won this fight when he wasn't immediately ushered to a wooden chair to meet the snipping sound of scissors wasn't approaching him from behind. My brother told my parents he would surely have his hair cut at school once he arrived; my father disagreed with this strategy and thought being prepared beforehand would give him a leg up with his superiors. In truth, Micheal shared with us siblings he wasn't ready to give up his identity. I think he was more scared than rebellious. Either way, the final days before his departure, my father asked him into the living room where his shaggy hair's fate was met.

Though Michael looked the part of a student with crisp, clean clothes and a fresh haircut, he was hardly ready to start school. His work ethic in school was always a discussion in the home which bled into his overall demeanor. He had trouble reading, which made learning and studying difficult for him. Testing at that time was almost nonexistent, making it difficult for my parents to distinguish his errant behavior from a true learning disability. Looking back now, I believe he must be dyslexic, but I've yet to confirm this theory.

My mother adored Michael and it was easy to tell that he was her favorite. Even when Michael grew up and moved away, my mother held on tight to him. She often interfered with his relationship with his wife, Suzanne.

There were just a few times when I strayed and needed their correction. A neighbor boy once called me over for a time of play. I rushed to his house only to find that his parents had purchased a toy for him that was identical to mine, except mine was beaten to a pulp from constant play over a couple of years. I used my powers of persuasion, knowing that I was bossy and big, to pressure him into giving me his toy. He folded easily and handed the new version of the toy to me. I returned home thrilled about my conquest.

When my parents found out, they weren't as proud of the Huckleberry Finn they were raising. They made me march back over to his house, assemble his entire family, and issue an apology speech. Then, not only was I to return the new toy to the neighbor, I had to hand over my old version of the toy as well.

I listened to my parents' teaching and was well-behaved and well-mannered most of the time. Unlike me, my brothers needed more attention. They never wanted to work with my father and I on big projects around the farm or go exploring in the forest. They just wanted to play all day. I loved the feeling of being industrious, sometimes helping to mow the property's fifteen acres. I loved being with my dad through it all.

In truth, I never sought the title of "favorite child" and didn't want to be compared to my brothers. It made me very uncomfortable and unhappy to know my mother had a favorite with Micheal. I had always questioned what he'd done, more perplexing what I hadn't, to receive her intense affections. However, it was clear when our parents sought the company of us children. I had felt most terribly for Ralph in our childhood. Perhaps that's why he acted as he did towards my mother's death. Maybe if my parents had treated us equally in their affections or quality time we'd all grow up close to one another. Back then, I had only known to turn off the jealousy by rebutting any notion I was a favorite of anyone. I certainly wasn't going to feed into that narrative about my father and I. It was obvious to everyone that my father preferred me, and such knowledge gave rise to nasty tempers. Especially in Ralph.

Although we were raised to think for ourselves, it shocked our parents when we began to stretch our wings as teenagers. I don't think they realized how fast we had grown. I remember my mother asking to speak with me about the years ahead when I was twelve. This was the only time we ever spoke like this. She had came into my room and told me about Christian Science. The teachings, what our family believed and why. This part was nothing new to me and when I heard her speak about criticizing truth and walking with compassion I felt it was the right thing to abide by. Easy. The next part was not as easy to swallow.

My mother was never crass, never judgmental – at least not outright—of other women's choices. However, when she told me I had to make a choice about the kind of woman I wanted to be, one who begs for attention or leads with her own intentions, I was confused to say the least.

Growing up, I was nothing less than a tomboy. I had no interest in love stories or playing house. My dolls did not marry. Instead, they hunted for food and discovered treasures. Even Fifi said it was a shame I was born a woman when I so clearly favored doing what other boys did. There was no desire to cater to anyone's desires but my own.

I looked at my mother as a deer greets headlights on the highway. She explained that I could waste my time appealing to the male gaze or stick to my path and eventually, a man worthy of my affection will simply run into me. She asked if I had any questions about sex and romance; it was more than obvious she did not want to discuss such things but the offer was quite kind. I replied that I did not. She left my room, and I went back to doing my math homework.

This interaction always perplexed me. Even now, as I try to imagine what she must have felt I can't help but chuckle a bit. I've never had daughters therefore I hold no judgment towards her position. She seemed to be taken off-guard that she'd have to hold such a conversation with me. I supposed this memory can be summed up as another moment my parents awkwardly tried to teach a lesson to their kids directly rather than let us learn by observation and experience.

Overall, my parents were hands-off as their children grew up. This was their blind spot. I see that now. When I watch my sons and their wives with my grandchildren, I can't help be think my parents could have spared some more affection towards us. Perhaps been a mentor in our experiences, especially by sharing more of their own. This was a part of their few faults. All parents have them — places where we lack objectivity about ourselves or our kids. That blind spot extended in my siblings' and my adult years.

Our parents believed that when their kids were eighteen and older, they needed to take charge of their lives without much help from them. I also see that was a tactical error as well. After experience and observation as one, I believe parenting is a lifelong obligation and the wisdom of a mother or father may grow even more necessary when kids get old.

This is not to discount the lifestyle my parents set forth for me. My father offered crucial advice to me often in my college years and occasionally shocked me by his willingness to open up as I aged. The way we see our parents is highly reflective of how we perceive our successes and failures; not to mention what we believe could have better with proper rearing.

Looking back, I only wish I could have had a relationship with my parents to ask them more questions about their experiences. Their emotions, and what caused them. In time, I may be able to do this.

And I heard a great voice out of heaven saying, Behold, the tabernacle of God is with men, and he will dwell with them, and they shall be his people, and God himself shall be with them, and be their God. And God shall wipe away all tears from their eyes; and there shall be no more death, neither sorrow, nor crying, neither shall there be any more pain: for the former things are passed away.
    Revelations 21:3-4

VIII.
DEATH KNOCKS

For weeks at a time, we would have to say goodbye to my father. He worked internationally in Egypt, Honduras, and other places globally. Most of his time was spent in Southern America, he worked as a consultant to a world-class expert in ceramics. We hated that he was gone for as long as he was and rejoiced when he returned.

It took him years of hard work and research to develop a line of ceramics sourced in the US. Most clay at the time came from China. Corona Industries, where he worked, wanted to become completely independent of imported products and my father was able to accomplish it.

One time, my mother and father went out to dinner with their friends. On the drive there, my mother went on and on about seeing the word "joy" on dishwashing liquid. My father would chide her about vibrating the air — his favorite phrase anytime any of us were pattering on. She never got offended. Mom knew how to laugh off his occasional cruelty.

Any gruffness he had was tempered by his affection for the family. And he was known for his good looks, charm, and wit. He was hopelessly in love with my mother and completely faithful to her.

He was an interesting man and did peculiar and lively things. Once, he got the idea to plant a pine forest. He dreamed those tiny six inch tall feathered sticks into majestic trees. In a few years, they were thirty feet tall.

My mother tried to get my brothers to stop playing long enough to join my father in these projects. They just wanted to do their own thing. I, on the other hand, shared my father's mentality about work mixed with fun while doing our little projects.

He gave his children a lot of latitude. We had the run of the town. If we wanted to go a few miles from home, we could. We lived in the cocoon of a community that kept children safe when all eyes were watching.

We are all products of our culture and upbringing. We can do all we can to escape the parts of our background we find less favorable. It's hard to separate one part from another and carve out a single section of our psyches. In reality, our history is a part of us and it can take a lifetime to scrub the subconscious mind clean of the things we now reject.

One thing I pray I never forget, however, is how deeply in love my parents were. They were the only parents I saw who kissed and hugged in public and around their kids. They were never secretive about their passion for one another and occasionally went slightly too far, putting on a bit of an inappropriate display for their youthful audience. Other children, including my brothers, snickered and acted queasy at the sight of their public displays of affection. I, though just as horrified by the sight, always secretly admired being the child of such affectionate parents. It gave me a sense of stability and wrapped me in a cocoon of love and safety.

My father would come home from work and my mother would put lipstick on to greet him. Then they'd share a drink. When times were tough, they sat together and drank sherry. When times were good, they drank martinis. Every day, they sat together and unwound the day.

Though I loved my mother dearly, she seemed to struggle with bouts of jealousy that I found distasteful, and I never wanted it to be a part of my character.

I saw these signs of jealousy with my mom for anyone my father cared about. She loved him so much, she seemed to want all his attention focused on her. Sometimes, her jealousy was justified, though. My father was out-going and good-looking. This often meant that he attracted unwanted attention from other ladies. Some were subtle with their flirting. Others were brazen and unashamed about trying to lure my father away from my mother. One of the worst offenders was my mother's third cousin, a woman whose husband suffered from some sort of sexual dysfunction, as I call it. The woman decided to hit on my father and my mother found out about it.

"You can't have my husband," my mother said, emphatically. She was not shy about putting women in their place when it came to her husband. That said, she had little to worry over. My father was in love with her and wouldn't risk his family for a one-night stand.

She was one of the greatest hostesses ever and would regularly host parties with beautiful decorations and delicious food. My father loved her parties and they were always the talk of the town.

Life was good, until, at the age of fifty, my dad was fired from his job. After all he had done to help the company and the money he saved them by bringing parts of the operations back to the US from China, they let him go with no notice or severance or retirement. He learned later that the reason for his random parting was due to the family-owned business's change in ownership. This new owner wanted only relatives working for them. It was a horrible shock to him since he had worked for the company all those years after the war.

People in those days retired at 55. That was not in his future. My parents had just built their home and now would have to sell it to support the family's future. The house was their dream, built with the finest materials under the best craftsmanship. It was a humbling experience to drive away from that house for the last time.

Dad bounced back by taking classes to improve his skills while working small jobs to support the family.

Then, to add insult to injury, when my mother's health started to fail, she insisted that my father stop working to take care of her. Admittedly, I had wished my mother had allowed my father to continue to work. Even if she couldn't go along with him on his trips, I felt then as I do now that she should have released him from the burden of her care. That said, I am empathetic to her emotions, as I sit now reminiscing on these thoughts from my bed. Too tired to do anything else than think of the past. My father's love for my mother would have moved heaven and earth – not without consequence, however. Giving up working harmed my father. I believe it contributed to his death.

I don't mean to judge their decision to sacrifice money for love. Things happen between a couple over the course of their relationship. We respond to them as best we can. Their marriage was most important to them above all. They sacrificed whatever they had to so that they could be together.

This is especially true when I consider how she spent her final days on earth. When mother was nearing her death, she laid in bed while my father crawled in beside her just to hold her hand. Often, he'd sit with her by the window, looking out over the green pastures. Truth be told, I think my father always loved my mother more than she loved him. He doted on her more than any other husband I've seen.

Perhaps the toughest lesson was that of grief and mourning. My mother fell ill often. Finally, though, she was so sick, there was no chance of her recovery.

A week before she died, my mother had the presence of mind to change her will because my brother, Ralph, stole $50,000 from her. She disinherited him even though she loved him dearly. She had said once that this did not mean he was completely lost. I however could not share as much optimism or enthusiasm for that future.

With that ugliness aside, she spent her final days with the loved ones. Towards the end, no one seemed to comfort her as much as my father. That was the only time I saw their love matched in intensity. She enjoyed his humor, his touch and the way he'd tend to her. This brought me immense joy as their daughter, and is another moment I wish I could ask her about what she thought and felt about the whole experience.

Her children rushed to the house to see her once more before she left us. By the time we arrived, my mother had died. Michael, my baby brother, and I hoped to secure a memento to remember her by. By the time we got there, Ralph, the second oldest and the one who had already stolen from my mother, returned and had plundered the estate. There was little left for us to have. I watched helplessly as my brothers got into an ugly confrontation that ended with Michael putting his hands around Ralph's throat and pushing him against a wall. I'd rather not go into more detail on this, as the anger and pain still sits with me.

Words fail to describe my father's grief. He was such a good man, I hated to see him suffer and have to face the rest of his life without his partner. My father was the sort of person who gave 101 percent to everything he did. He had the capacity to enjoy life in ways others envied. He didn't care much about a person's race, gender, or color. He embraced everyone. I went to visit my father every year after my mother passed away. I wanted to spend as much time with him as I could. He lived a year and a month after my mother's passing. Today, my brothers regret that they didn't spend more time with him. At least, I know Micheal does.

I thank my God upon every remembrance of you,
   Always in every prayer of mine for you all making request with joy,
   For your fellowship in the gospel from the first day until now;
   Being confident of this very thing, that he which hath begun a good work in you will perform it until the day of Jesus Christ:
   Even as it is meet for me to think this of you all, because I have you in my heart; inasmuch as both in my bonds, and in the defence and confirmation of the gospel, ye all are partakers of my grace.
   Phillipians 1:3-7

IX.

COLLEGE FEMINITY

In the tradition of the bright women in my family, I made plans to leave home in search of a college education. This is the expected path for women today. Unsurprisingly, in the days of my youth, the men worked and the women stayed home to have and raise babies. Going off to college was a bold rejection of the norm. Anyone who knew me, however, should have known that was not the path I would take. I felt that the whole world was laid out for me like a gourmet meal on a platter. I would taste it all.

I took to college like a fish to water. The academics fit me well. Socializing was a bit harder to adapt to.

Making friends with women was especially hard. For starters, I grew up with mostly boys. Plus, we lived way out in the country, making it tough to connect with a large number of girls. And there was no distinction between boys and girls when I was young in terms of what we were allowed to do. I was encouraged to try everything my brothers did by both parents, which I think is what truly encouraged me to break the normative of what a woman should do and say. I was never shooed away or told to go inside and cook something, unless I fancied that skill! Because of that, I would swing an ax, handle a gun, shoot an arrow, and play – aggressively. I participated in all their sports. I owned my own skis, skates, sleds, and hockey pucks. Most of all, I was physically different from most girls, standing almost six feet tall by the age of thirteen.

In sixth grade, a girl named Carol made it her mission to outshine everyone else, especially me. She wanted to be number one, and anyone who stood in her way was met with thinly veiled hostility. Carol was competitive and determined to a fault, so when our paths crossed in sports, she hated it. She hated me! I was stronger and faster, and that didn't sit well with her. She seemed to harbor a special kind of disdain for me, one that she didn't display to others. Thankfully, I had friends who made those days brighter. We were a quirky bunch, bonded over a shared love for science fiction, MAD magazine, and the odd pastime of eating whole onions for sport. We were not part of the popular clique, but we didn't care.

My mother did care. She was concerned about my social development and decided that ballroom dancing might be the key to improving my social skills. I don't know if it was by design or mere coincidence, but the dance instructor often paired me with the shorter boys in the class. I towered over them awkwardly and I was a bad dancer, constantly tripping over my own feet and struggling to follow the steps. The experience was meant to be a remedy for my social awkwardness, but instead, it highlighted it in new and uncomfortable ways.

My mother should have known that I would be different from the average kid. I was a unique child from the start of my life. I think my mother had a hint before I was born. When she was pregnant with me she'd tell others she could feel it was a boy. Of course, I quickly became the apple of my parents' eye, but there was something about her pregnancy that made her think she was carrying a male. That, coupled with my personality by age three, which provoked Fifi to make similar comments about my misplaced gender pairing, the lore of my mother's intuition during pregnancy became an unconscious but never negative thought. Fortunately, she got a rough-and-tumble female.

Other signs of my unique personality emerged over my toddler years. At two years of age, I would stand in the middle of adult conversations listening and taking in all the words, hand gestures, and facial expressions. I was always interested in people and found them fascinating to watch, so engaging with them was easy

My interests were not in filling doll houses with furniture and playing the marriage games other little girls played. I wanted to be "out there" doing what my dad did and letting my curiosity take me where it wanted to.

I expected college would be easy for me academically because I had been a stellar student, scoring A's in all of my classes throughout my schooling. I loved learning as much as I loved being at home with my family. School was my home away from home.

My parents pushed me to excel with lots of encouragement. At times, though, my father's encouragement bordered on insane perfectionism. When I brought home a paper to show him how well I had done, I beamed with pride at the "100" that the teacher had scrawled across the top of the paper. My father would smile down and me and joke, "Why didn't you get 105?" That said, his tone still had a ring of true disappointment.

I could have easily graduated from high school at the age of twelve if I had been given access to the right education and the resources given to other gifted children in the main cities. I had been blessed with a good brain. School was easy; I barely had to work hard at it. That same mastery followed me into college.

Again, college and I got along very well in terms of my studies. Socially, I was shy and a bit awkward, making other girls wary of me. Worse, one of my cousins who also came from money was spoiled with an abundant amount of clothing, which she would ship me frequently. I would receive gifts of expensive, designer clothing as hand-me-downs. Funny thing to complain about, but with a hoard of eyes already on you, adding any reason for a target on your back glued by jealousy was not the smartest idea. Looking back, I suppose it was better I was gawked at while strutting with fashion instead of the boots and boy shorts I'd wear at home.

At Alfred University, I had a roommate for the first time at, where I lived in a dorm called the Brick. It was there that I experienced discrimination for the first time. None of the guys asked me out because they were Jewish and only dated Jewish girls, a reality that left me feeling excluded despite not seeing race. To keep myself busy and entertained, I would take my saxophone to the Top Castle and play at night. That's how I spent my early college days, immersing myself in music with the band and studying hard. I don't often speak much about my saxophone talents, although it was a skill I acquired around my preteen years and adored playing in my downtime with my father. I took to it much more once I went to the University.

There were few girls to interact with in school as it was largely populated by African men. I dated many of them much to the chagrin of the few Jewish girls who were there.

One man in particular stood six-foot-five and came to pick me up for a date. He was a vision of charm, intelligence, and good looks. I noticed how strangely people looked at me as this freakishly tall white girl dating this huge African vision of handsomeness. This was 1962 when interracial dating was nothing close to accepted. From my earliest college days, I was open to all kinds of people and never found anything wrong with being attracted to whoever I was attracted to. I followed my heart... and admittedly sometimes my hormones as well.

The date started formally as he picked me up from my building. I signed myself out and he promised to bring me back by curfew. We walked to whatever destination we were headed to but never arrived. If you asked me to explain this story in my youth, maybe even thirty years ago, I'd say he was very aggressive and got physical too soon. He wanted to kiss me before we even had our dinner! When I rejected him, he insisted and grabbed my arms. This being my first date with any man, along with my already ignorance in how to handle a situation like this with anyone I told him to pound sand and raced back home. I never went out with him again. Looking back at this now, I find my reaction and the whole event more humorous than anything else.

I can't explain why, but that night made me decide that I should join a sorority. I suppose my logic was tossing myself into the mouth of female lions would teach me more about how to become one myself. That said, I wasn't going to join just any house with girls who clearly thought only about their looks and impressing men more than their brains. After all, I was still a major nerd.

After scrutiny, I found a community of more open-minded girls to befriend. They were more interested in ideas about the world than the prim and proper girls of other sororities. After getting to know them, I learned that they had been exposed to all kinds of people in their lives. They had Black friends of their own and didn't consider me peculiar for dating outside of my race. They thought about how to better themselves physically, emotionally, and spiritually – most girls coming from Christian homes. They invested themselves in politics and loved to debate with anyone. It was like God created these women for a tall nerd with no social skills! We could talk and laugh without worry of offending each other.

My sorority sisters accepted me for who I was and liked me just as I was. They appreciated that I was brave and admired me for my lifestyle choices. They had adventurous spirits as well and were secure in themselves. Fear of other people's opinions or peer pressure didn't intimidate them.

As I met more people, I gravitated to those in my community who proved themselves to be more seasoned and less conservative. They weren't taught to hate or exclude. They liked to have a good time in life. They certainly had more robust senses of humor. Most of all, their curiosity about life was attractive to me. When they saw someone who was different, they were interested rather than repelled. They were my tribe.

Even though I continued to be somewhat insecure socially, I knew what I liked and wasn't about to avoid someone because of a superficial difference. Even though I had found a good group of friends, I continued to struggle as I interacted with others in my classes and other times when I wasn't in the safety of my social circle. As a result, I don't remember those days with fondness and didn't enjoy college very much. The classes were tough. The labs were long. I had to compete with the guys who had 20-year records of the past tests. Worse, I struggled in calculus. My professor (who, coincidentally taught my father) only offered two grades: A or F. It cast a shadow over my whole college career.

That said, over time I grew to learn the art of man. I learned how to talk, flirt, and receive courtship. Sounds silly to say, but when you don't have a mentor in such things in early life, you learn as an adult. There is an art to romance, another thing one does not appreciate until they are confronted with it. Objectively, I became very good at said art and thoroughly enjoyed dating. So much so, I didn't have the desire to have a serious relationship immediately. The most serious relationships I had at that time was with my close girlfriends; whom, nine times out of ten, were favorable to that of the opposite sex.

One of the great blessings of college, however, was the friendship I made with a woman named Naomi. She and I went out for coffees together just about every day in the beginning of our relationship. It grew and grew until we were spending most of our free time together.

Naomi was bright, funny, and loved art, music, and all the things I loved. We could talk about Broadway, compare notes about men, and scout out ways we could have fun. Best of all, I didn't tower over her. Naomi was 6'1." Like me, she was interested in ideas more than ideology.

Naomi and I spent a lot of time together. Sometimes, our outings stretched into the night. The dormitory I lived in required girls to sign in and out so they knew all the girls came home each night. During one of our late night, I decided that I would sleep over at Naomi's house, which was against school rules. I was placed on social probation. It was the second time I had been placed on probation. The first infraction was during my sexual revolution. I met a guy and brought him back to my dormitory. While we were having sex, the fire alarm sounded. We got caught as we were escaping the building. Naomi got a great laugh when she heard.

Naomi was a committed vegetarian. Fortunately, there were plenty of places we could eat. The food in the area was out of this world sourced from local markets that provided bread, vegetables, and fruit. Naomi was also a great cook, so we ate well whether we went out to eat or hunkered down for a night of fun at her place. She was a true friend throughout my college years and beyond. When I lost my job after college, Naomi opened her doors to me, giving me a place to stay in the apartment she'd rented while pursuing her master's degree.

Her place was tiny. The bathroom and kitchen were combined. They were called railroad apartments or tub-in-the-kitchen apartments because there was literally a bright red bathtub resting against the kitchen wall. Sounds pretty East Coast. I lived there for two months while saving enough for my own place.

Within two weeks of losing my job, I got hired. A couple of months later, I found an apartment of my own. I knew it was important not to wear out my welcome by staying at her home too long. Noami wasn't one to say anything but I always hated the feeling of sticking around when I could give someone space. Not to mention the freedom of living alone after spending years stuck in a dorm room or house with other women was godsend.

Naomi and I were like sisters. We spent all our time together, barely noticing until others pointed it out. We went to every party together, laughed together, and cried together. When we weren't working or studying, we cruised the streets for guys together. Unfortunately, most of the guys we liked were gay. So, we opted for concerts, walking through the park, and sightseeing our little world.

We were at one party where the hosts positioned dry ice everywhere, creating clouds beneath our feet. There was a lot of smoke in the air as well as people puffed on cigarettes and marijuana. I wasn't terribly interested in smoking, but just being in the room was enough to get a contact high. This was how it was at many of the parties we attended. Two six foot tall wall flowers, sitting on the floor, people-watching.

At another party, we sat on the floor, talking and observing. Lots of folks around us were doing all kinds of drugs. Naomi and I just sat together, each of us knowing without having to say it that we weren't going to let each other indulge and risk getting hooked. Besides, we weren't there for a high; we were there to find men.

That night, something curious happened. At one point in the evening, our eyes met. There was such a comfort and connection between us that some sort of strange energy passed between us. When we talked about it later, we were shocked to learn that we were both asking the same two questions: "Am I gay" and "Are we supposed to be together?"

Of course, it would likely make my story more riveting if I included a sapphic romance that lasted for years before starting my family. Surely would sell more copies these days. Alas, that isn't what happened. We laughed and agreed that the connection between us didn't feel lustful, surely kismet nonetheless. This started a longer discussion about the dynamics of a relationship and why two people do fall in love. It was that experience that made me question the type of marriage I'd eventually want and wife I'd want to be.

Naomi, like me, was brave. She had the courage to think deeply about life and who she was. As it turned out, we both got married and had children, having dated only men all our lives. But we understood something about having a bond with another woman that made love feel universal.

We were certainly stronger together than we were apart. Having her by my side made it easier to make friends. We embraced people of all colors, genders, faiths, etc.

We talked about the important issues of our time openly, discussing our stand on the events happening in the world: civil rights, the American Indian Movement, the Stonewall, and the gay rights movement. We challenged the orthodoxy and hypocrisy in religion. And we marched!

No topic was bigger than the Vietnam War. It was a hot-button issue for us because we actually knew people who went to war.

Naomi and I had a Black friend who served in Vietnam. After the war, we ran into him while walking in the park. He was so damaged by the war, he was just a shell of the man he was before he left. We chatted with him for a few minutes before walking away and deciding that we could no longer befriend him. It broke our hearts. It was clear that he was on the edge of hurting others and would not be safe to be around. At that time, there weren't strong resources to help veterans like there are now, and even so, the sources are lacking in efficiency. We made the best choice we knew. The war had dimmed the light in his eyes and broken everything that was strong and confident in him. He was a dangerous combination of nervous, angry, and afraid. The war had taken all but his heartbeat.

Naomi and I went on to be friends the rest of our lives, speaking on and off, sharing stories of our families, and continuing our sister-like friendship. Perhaps in another life I could have offered a juicier story filled with lesbian affairs– sorry Penguin Publishing.

Take heed that ye do not your alms before men, to be seen of them: otherwise ye have no reward of your Father which is in heaven.

Therefore when thou doest thine alms, do not sound a trumpet before thee, as the hypocrites do in the synagogues and in the streets, that they may have glory of men. Verily I say unto you, They have their reward.

But when thou doest alms, let not thy left hand know what thy right hand doeth:

That thine alms may be in secret: and thy Father which seeth in secret himself shall reward thee openly.

And when thou prayest, thou shalt not be as the hypocrites are: for they love to pray standing in the synagogues and in the corners of the streets, that they may be seen of men. Verily I say unto you, They have their reward.

But thou, when thou prayest, enter into thy closet, and when thou hast shut thy door, pray to thy Father which is in secret; and thy Father which seeth in secret shall reward thee openly.

But when ye pray, use not vain repetitions, as the heathen do: for they think that they shall be heard for their much speaking.

Be not ye therefore like unto them: for your Father knoweth what things ye have need of, before ye ask him.

Matthew 6:1-8

X. LADY LIBERATION

I find myself hard-pressed to think of anything that proved more transformative for young college women of my generation than the development of the birth control pill. When the pill arrived on the scene in the early 1960s, it didn't just change individual lives; it revolutionized an entire culture. Everyone, and I truly mean everyone, started having sex, including me. It was as if women had collectively acknowledged what we had always known but rarely admitted: that our greatest fear was not intimacy itself, but the specter of unwanted pregnancy and the social ruin that accompanied having a baby out of wedlock.

The pill, approved by the FDA in 1960, represented more than mere contraception. It was liberation in a small, round package. Once that primal fear of pregnancy was virtually eradicated, we seized our newfound sexual freedom with the desperation of drowning souls clutching life preservers. This wasn't just personal liberation, it was part of a broader cultural awakening that historians would later call the Sexual Revolution. The pill gave women control over their reproductive destiny for the first time in human history, and with that control came choices that previous generations could never have imagined.

It unleashed a kind of freedom we could hardly contain, awakening the sexual vitality that had been suppressed and pent up in all of us for generations. I went wild, as did countless women of my time. We were part of a generation that would redefine what it meant to be a woman in America, challenging every assumption about female sexuality, ambition, and autonomy.

Women of my era, and I suspect those of my mother's and grandmother's generations, had been raised with a fundamentally different understanding of sexuality. We weren't taught that sex was something to be savored or enjoyed. We weren't supposed to derive pleasure from it; we were simply expected to endure it. Our roles had been clearly defined and rigidly enforced: satisfy our husbands and produce children. The Victorian notion that "good women" didn't enjoy sex had persisted well into the twentieth century, creating generations of women who approached intimacy with duty rather than desire.

With the advent of the pill, however, we could finally evaluate what we genuinely liked and didn't like sexually, freed from the constant anxiety of conception. I embraced this opportunity wholeheartedly. I had boyfriends from time to time and felt no reservations about having sex with them. Marriage held no appeal for me. I didn't want that kind of constrained life where I would be tied down to domestic expectations and social conventions. I still craved adventure, still yearned for experiences that would challenge and change me. I understood instinctively that traditional marriage would create a barrier between me and the wider world that beckoned, the world where I intended to carve out my own unique place.

When I imagined my life projected like a movie on the big screen, I was never cast in the role of the damsel in distress, languishing in a flowing gown, peering anxiously from behind curtains while waiting for some hero to return home. Nor was I the helpless captive trapped in a tower, hoping desperately that a knight would appear on the horizon, colors flying, vowing to rescue me or die in the attempt. In the vivid picture that played continuously in my mind, I was the protagonist of my own story. I was the hero of my own adventure.

I recognized that achieving such a life would require sacrifices, that I would have to forgo many of the things that traditional women of my generation were taught to want and expect. The truth was, I didn't have a single boyfriend whom I wanted to marry, even though I could have easily married any one of them. What I wanted instead was profoundly different: to work in a meaningful career, to earn and control my own money, and to have the freedom to pursue enjoyment and fulfillment on my own terms.

Though I embraced sexual freedom, I discovered that sex held little interest for me unless I was genuinely in love or cared deeply for my partner. Casual encounters seemed foreign and unsatisfying to me. I had no interest in one-night stands or intimacy with strangers. The men I chose to be with were individuals who truly attracted me, not just physically but intellectually and emotionally. They were fascinating people who accepted me completely for who I was, men who weren't intimidated or threatened by my strength, my intelligence, or my unconventional ambitions.

It was crucial that I only shared intimacy with people who allowed me to remain authentically myself. I knew countless women who went to extraordinary lengths to conceal their intelligence, to dim their intellectual light in order to appear more appealing to men. Many men of our generation simply couldn't handle a genuinely intelligent woman. While such attitudes would be considered unconscionable today, back then, women routinely "dumbed themselves down" just to secure a date. The harsh reality was that if they didn't, men would be turned off and seek someone who seemed less intellectually challenging. Brilliant women were viewed as threatening rather than desirable, making it infinitely more difficult for women who wanted to find husbands and start families. They felt compelled to hide their most valuable qualities out of fear of being alone.

This social dynamic profoundly shaped my perception of what it meant to be a woman in America. I instinctively and completely rejected that notion. I understood that my refusal to diminish myself would make it more difficult to find a compatible partner, but I had to remain true to myself and always maintain my authenticity. I simply didn't know any other way to exist in the world. From my earliest memories, I had presented myself exactly as I was, without pretense or performance. I had always been completely transparent, a what-you-see-is-what-you-get person from the youngest age. My character and personality had been formed and honed from the very beginning of my conscious life. Besides, my mother had wisely told me that the person I was meant to be with would not be found standing on any ordinary street corner. He would be someone exceptional, someone rare. He would have to be.

I mistakenly believed I had discovered that special person when my Psychology professor began showing romantic interest in me. He invited me out for dinner, bought me drinks, and what I initially perceived as an exciting, if unconventional, relationship quickly transformed into something much darker and more troubling. The affair itself was initially quite pleasant, embodying everything one might read about in the problematic romance novels of today that feature an older man and a younger woman, complete with a superficially satisfying happy ending. Needless to say, the reality ended disastrously. I was a senior, standing on the very brink of graduation, when the professor's predatory nature became impossible to ignore or rationalize away.

When my father discovered what had happened, his reaction surprised me with its composure and grace. He drove to the college to pick me up, took me to a quiet restaurant, ordered me a martini and a proper lunch, and calmly advised me not to marry young. He never once raised his voice or expressed anger. Instead, he asked gently if I wanted to come home to collect myself and recover from the ordeal. He told me I was welcome to make whatever decision felt right to me, but if I chose to return to school, I would do so with my head held high, finishing my education with dignity regardless of what anyone else might say or think about me.

This response was such a profound surprise. It marked the first and truly the only time I ever experienced my father as a genuine safe haven, at least in this particular way. He had always been so devoted to my mother, so focused on her needs and desires, that this moment felt like a precious taste of what she must have felt from him regularly: complete trust, absolute acceptance, and unconditional love. My mother, however, never quite treated me the same way after this incident, maintaining a subtle distance that persisted even until her death. I also wish I could say that the University's reaction proved equally understanding and supportive. My father's cool, measured demeanor stood in stark contrast to their harsh and punitive response.

Word of the affair spread across campus with the speed and viciousness of wildfire. I was immediately expelled for an entire semester for what the administration deemed "inappropriate behavior." I was treated like a social pariah, shunned and whispered about wherever I went. I had no choice but to return home in shame. I found work at a local coffee shop and kept my head down, focusing on saving money and surviving each day. My strategy during this period of academic probation was to attract as little attention to myself as possible, to become invisible until I could return to school. I worked diligently every day, and when the time finally came for me to return to my studies, I shot out of my childhood home like a racehorse leaving the stables for the first time, desperate for freedom and redemption.

Returning to school felt like walking directly into a battlefield, arriving with my tail between my legs and my reputation in tatters. The Dean of Women had labeled me a threat to the moral fabric of society, expressing genuine fear that I would somehow contaminate other girls with my scandalous behavior. It was an extraordinarily harsh and deeply humiliating period of my life. Even though sharing a room with another student could be enjoyable and provided built-in companionship, most girls preferred single rooms because they made it easier to secretly invite boys over for nights of passion and intimacy. However, when I returned to college, there was absolutely no difficulty securing a single room because no one wanted to be my roommate. It was as if I wore Hawthorne's scarlet letter, marked and branded for all to see.

I felt completely defenseless and profoundly ashamed. This became a crucial decision point in my young life. I could either cower in that shame, allowing it to define and diminish me, or I could prove myself to be the capable, resilient woman I knew myself to be. It was my father's words of encouragement and support that gave me the courage to choose the latter path. For the remainder of that semester, I threw myself completely into my studies, made curfew every single night without exception, and never went out on a date with any boy until after graduation. Not that any actually asked me out during that time. I had become known as "the tall tart who even dated the black boys," a reputation that made me completely untouchable in the social hierarchy of the early 1960s.

Despite the social isolation and constant humiliation, I excelled academically in all my classes and graduated at the very top of my class. Ironically, this academic success only made the scandals surrounding me more sensational and appealing to campus gossips. Meanwhile, my professor and former lover was merely sent on a brief leave of absence before returning to his teaching position as if nothing had ever happened. We never spoke again after news of our affair became public knowledge, our silence a testament to the different consequences we faced for the same relationship.

*L*ove must be sincere. Hate what is evil; cling to what is good.
Be devoted to one another in love. Honor one another above yourselves.
Never be lacking in zeal, but keep your spiritual fervor, serving the Lord.
Be joyful in hope, patient in affliction, faithful in prayer.
Share with the Lord's people who are in need. Practice hospitality.
Romans 12:9-13

XI.
FOR LOVE

I believe we are each owed at least one great romance in our lifetimes. Sometimes, benevolence blesses us with more. There is nothing sweeter than loving and being loved completely by someone. That is what I thought I had found in Charles.

I met Charles on the corner of Shadock Avenue, where he pulled up next to me in his Volkswagen and asked if I wanted a ride. Blinded by love and lust, I climbed in, completely spellbound.

Charles was a Black jazz musician and a real estate broker, a bass player whose passion for music matched my own. We fell in love, got married, and had two children, creating a life together on East 19th Street in Oakland. Eventually, we bought a house in Hayward, CA, to make my commute to a job in Silicon Valley more manageable, though it was still a 60-mile trek each way.

For a while, life was beautiful. We played music together all the time, and I learned so much from him. We didn't have the same union as my parents, although he did make me feel alive. He was also extremely attractive, which I admit now with a smile was a major bonus in being married to him. Soon, the harmony was fleeting. Charles was quick to change—he became controlling and jealous, wanting to dominate me completely. Nothing I did was ever good enough. His legalistic way of keeping track of every argument, his drug use, and his deep-seated fear and misogyny created an increasingly toxic environment.

Despite the growing turmoil, I stayed with him too long. As a scientist, I believed anything could be healed. That said, it was obvious to me at that time that Charles didn't really love me; he didn't care about anyone. After our divorce, I found myself out of a job and spent $2,000 on career counseling, desperate to avoid losing my house. He had stolen and pawned my treasured saxophones, and I received no child support. Yet, despite everything, I eventually forgave him. It is a divine truth to forgive and I still believe that though my marriage to him was unfortunate, he blessed me with two lives I'd never regret being apart of my sons, Charles and Stephen. He also taught me a tremendous amount about love, lessons about which I have kept close to me as I went on in my life after our divorce.

He hasn't changed much in all these years, but enough to be happy for him and look back at our youth and time together with a smile. We still have a good relationship and my sons are kind to him; they don't resent him. This matters most to me now.

After Charles and I split, I met Gene. My relationship with Gene was fulfilling, fun, lustful, and full of life. He was odd like me when we were young. He was from Hong Kong and had darker skin than his peers. He appeared almost Mongolian. He was also tall, my neck hadn't felt such rest in years! He and I shared a dark sense of humor which drew us to each other. We will be friends forever. I was genuinely happy with him and am not afraid to say he is the love of my life. If we had gotten married, it would have been splendid with me. He taught me new things like how to sail, and shared my love for travel. He treated me with respect and we had deep discussions about everything you can think of.

When you become an older woman, who has spent so much of her life caring for others, learning, sacrificing your time and energy on bettering yourself or simply proving yourself to others who frankly don't equal your talents, you start to relish in the serenity of quiet. Of contentment. That's how I felt with Gene. He and I were enough. He wanted to have children with me and I was just content with us. It is not in my nature to be a burden, nor to hold onto that which is not mine. After many talks, I knew that as much as I'd love a child with Gene, I was beyond that time in my life. I was ready for another chapter. We thought it best to break up. This was a true heartbreak for both of us.

We have connected occasionally over the years and I've gotten to see photos of his wife and children. He's so filled with light and happiness in every memory he shares with me. Though I still think about a life I could have lived with him, I believe true love is non-possessive. There is nothing but love and admiration for him still.

As I grew older and continued to date, I found it increasingly challenging. Older men often sought a nursemaid more than a romantic partner, and those in good health were obsessed with sex, preferring younger women. They weren't raised to have friendships with women outside of sex, which made finding a genuine connection difficult.

Throughout my life, there has been a recurring theme of wanting to please others. It is one of the great contradictions in my personality; despite living a life counter to the norm, I yearned for approval. This desire almost always worked to my detriment. Charles knew this flaw and exploited it, controlling me by seizing on my insecurities. He knew I would work tirelessly to fix anything that didn't please him, only for him to find something else to criticize once I did. Gene allowed me peace but was at another stage in life than myself.

In the end, my relationships with Charles and Gene taught me invaluable lessons about love, self-worth, and resilience. They revealed the importance of self-acceptance and the dangers of seeking validation from others. While I continue to believe in the sweetness of a great romance, I also understand that the greatest love story is the one we have with ourselves.

I tried to maintain good relationships with the men of my past. In fact, one of my old boyfriends reconnected with me after many years. He is having some health challenges. He is happily married to a wonderful woman and has a lovely daughter who is very accomplished. He is still active and enjoys skiing with his family. We are still good friends after all these years. There is nothing but love and friendship between us.

These interactions make me smile at life's unexpectedness. To be known by someone for decades is gratifying. We simply cannot choose how our stories will play out but to see how some of mine have is an astonishing experience.

The following is an excerpt by Charles Brigham Sr.:

Kris and I met in Oakland California at a Lake Merritt health food store that she managed. I went there to buy vitamins and saw her at the check stand with a big smile on her face. I was done.

We dated for a while and at that time, she was in transition from New York to Oakland. We enjoyed many deep and fulfilling conversations and fun outdoor activities. She taught me how to sail a sailboat, we went to the beach frequently, and we studied music together. We also did a little camping in the Redwoods with our children, Charles and Stephan while living in Oakland and Hayward together.

Kris was a gifted artist and musician. Most of all, she was a Spiritual gift to all the people she loved and those who knew her. She taught me how to see the good and value in others, what it means to seek Spiritual growth and commitment, and to love cats!

Kris was a truly gifted scientist committed to working and spirituality, and she lived it.

Ultimately, I was married to one of the greatest Queens of the Universe and that is the reason I never married again.

I'll love her always.

Our Father which art in heaven, Hallowed be thy name.

Thy kingdom come, Thy will be done in earth, as it is in heaven.
Give us this day our daily bread.
And forgive us our debts, as we forgive our debtors.
And lead us not into temptation, but deliver us from evil: For thine is the kingdom, and the power, and the glory, for ever.
Amen.
Matthew 6: 9-13

XII.
SAIL ON

I was the only one out of four women to make it through engineering school, a testament to my perseverance and determination. Despite this achievement, finding a job proved to be an even greater challenge. In an era where bias was rampant, my qualifications seemed to matter less than my gender. To navigate this, I changed my name to "Kris" on my resume. I thought it would lead employers to assume I was male and I would at least be able to get a foot in the door.

At nearly six feet tall and strikingly attractive, I left quite an impression when I arrived for interviews and men saw that I was female. Employers' jaws would drop, not with admiration, but with a realization that they had assumed wrong.

One memorable experience was my first interview at RCA in Lancaster, Pennsylvania. I took the Greyhound bus, filled with hope and ambition, only to find that all the male candidates received job offers while I did not.

Undeterred, I kept pushing forward. My persistence paid off. I was hired as a research chemist by a company in Morristown, New Jersey. At 21, driving my first car, a 1967 Mustang, I felt a mix of excitement and trepidation. Morristown was not the ideal place for a young woman embarking on her professional journey, but it was a start. This job was just a stepping stone.

Entering the workforce as a freshly minted engineering graduate was like stepping into a battlefield, armed with nothing but my intellect and determination to succeed. In a field, dominated by men, I was acutely aware of the challenges that lay ahead—a reality that would test my resolve and force me to confront the biases and prejudices that permeated the corporate world.

At my new job in Morristown, New Jersey, I faced a critical decision: be true to myself as a woman or adopt the mentality and behaviors of the men around me. I observed the workplace dynamics and saw that the successful women acted like their male colleagues. They just wanted to blend in and thrive in a male-dominated environment.

I made a different choice. I decided to go my own way and remain authentic regardless of the consequences. This decision came with a heavy price.

In the world of technology and engineering, many lies were told, from overstated capabilities to false promises. That said, I never lied. My honesty made me a target. My bosses hated me for it and saw my integrity as a threat to their agendas. Despite my success in solving numerous problems, my straightforwardness and refusal to play the game made me unpopular with the higher-ups.

I remember an encounter with my boss in the hallway, where he asked me about some processes. I answered truthfully, knowing full well that he wouldn't like my responses. Each answer I gave was pushing me closer to the exit door, but I stood by my principles.

It only took ten months before I was let go. The official reason was that the company had decided my work was no longer their focus, but I knew the truth. My refusal to compromise my integrity, my choice to remain honest and authentic, had cost me my job.

The stress of this conflict, the constant battle to maintain my values in a hostile environment, took a toll on my health. I attribute my heart problems to that time. I was under constant emotional and psychological strain. The day I was fired, I felt a mix of relief and defeat. I had stayed true to myself, but at a significant personal cost.

After that, I started working for a dot.com startup, alongside some of the smartest people I'd ever met. One man got his Ph.D. from Stanford while he was in his freshman year of college. He was a wonderfully odd and brilliant man named John. I can still see him with his crazy look because his brain was always in motion.

As a material scientist, I had experience with chip making and worked to make them smaller and denser. They had been searching for someone with those skills and hired me immediately. The staff was small but mighty. They were all interesting and strange characters like me and I felt like I had found my tribe of scientists and chemists. We worked seven days a week, putting in fifteen hours per day typically.

I was known at work for my earrings that were designed by Naomi. One of my co-workers called me "Barbie" because of the beautiful earrings I wore each day. It amused me to receive such a nickname since I was the last person who should have been associated with Barbie. I didn't play with dolls, though my grandmother tried her best to get me interested in them. She gave me exquisite dolls throughout my childhood that I ignored.

Along with the new work placement, I had to change my living arrangements, a fun tangent. I initially rented a room close to the office, which had me living with a somewhat sex-obsessed guy. Though he was never forward or inappropriate with me, he had designed a Playboy area in the front of his house that I had to pass through that area each day to get to my room. Needless to say, I couldn't wait to get a place of my own.

I worked at this place for four years, commuting from my rented room with a sex-obsessed man to the office in San Jose for the first nine months. Eventually, I was able to buy a condo in San Francisco. Though I was working every day, I knew that I had to have a life outside of the office. Of course, this was easier once I moved out and on my own again.

Hewlett-Packard had offered me a month's salary for every year I worked there, which was fourteen years. I left Palo Alto with a stack of cash that I used to buy the condo in San Francisco. I moved into an area where many entrepreneurs in the dot.com boom lived. The energy was so electric, it seemed as if I could reach out and touch it. And there I was right in the center of all that was exciting and new. New city, new home, and a new job. All I needed was new hobby... and perhaps a new man.

I started searching for Don Riley, the only leader of a racing crew of sailors made up of only women. I wanted to join this crew and race. Though my father was a water lover, he hadn't taught me to sail, so I had a lot to learn. Fortunately, the time we spent in the ocean made it like a second home I longed to return to.

I registered for sailing lessons and built a great relationship with my instructor. The instructor was clearly attracted to me. He told me that there were essentially two kinds of sailors: the hard drinkers or the womanizers. My instructor warned me of both, probably to win my favor so that I would date a safe bet like him. I liked him too, but the sparks never lit between us. So, we never developed a romantic relationship and settled for the joy of sailing together.

Every Friday and as often as I could, I went to the club to be in the heart of the sailing community. It was nice to cruise up and down the bay; but my heart yearned to make those boats fly!

I got involved in sailboat racing in Berkeley, sailing in the San Francisco Bay. Being in the water and fast racing thrilled me. But, if I'm honest. I thought I would find a love interest in the sailing community. Sadly, and much to my surprise, there was a culture of polyamory there that I would not get involved in. Turns out this is common in sailing communities. Despite being alive in the 70's and a huge advocate (and tester) for birth control, I did not want to participate. So, I did not find the love of my life in that community.

I immersed myself in sailing, showing up to the races to see if anyone was looking for crewmates; there was always a boat in need of more crew. I got to race on different boats before joining a small yacht club in San Francisco. Some captains were great. They were motivating and appreciative. Others were mean as junkyard dogs. They yelled and screamed at their crew and were never satisfied with the work people did. Their only objective was winning and could care less if their crew had a moment's fun. The best scenario was to have your own boat so that you could create the kind of environment best for you.

I was overjoyed when my good friend, Emmanuel, offered me a partnership in a boat in San Francisco. It was a gorgeous cruiser we called "The Winnebago of the Bay." We developed a rotating schedule so everyone could enjoy cruising up and down the peninsula. Emmanuel and I often cruised together, fighting 20-knot winds.

I passionately loved sailing. The South Beach Yacht Club, which is now quite famous, had a host of great members. I met a man named Richard who owned a great boat. I loved racing Richard. Every Friday night, we went out racing or sailing. I had this fantasy that I would someday meet someone and start a romantic relationship at the Yacht Club. After all, I was surrounded by men. And since there were very few female sailors, I thought my odds were pretty good. I later learned that my instructor was not exactly telling me the truth. The stereotype was that sailors were serial monogamists who "grew up" to be family men. Not true. This is another shocking truth I learned while sailing. What a great pond to fish in.

I sailed all over including the British Virgin Islands where we chartered a boat for a sailing vacation. We had amazing times, but I didn't meet the love of my life there but I did make many friends.

There were a few women who enjoyed racing and I was able to form great friendships in the boat racing community. It was one of the joys of my life.

My philosophy was to enjoy life. I was willing to put in the training and work that was necessary to do these activities. It was hard work, but it was worth it. Beyond sailing and the archery, rifles, and axes of my youth, I also stood at the top of glaciers. It's an experience that defied explanation. I remember standing there on the summit, looking out for hundreds of miles.

Again, there were a few women who craved such adventures. I would be in the stores buying skis, boots, snowshoes, and backpacks, and as I looked around the store, I would see that I was the only woman there. I felt like a duck pretending to be a crocodile. Looking back, I was more like a Swan amongst ducklings. I flourished in those environments and became comfortable being underestimated in any environment.

Sadly, I got too weak to continue this lifestyle. I had done what I enjoyed for so long, I had no regrets. I had great memories and a fabulous job soon after. Sometimes I wonder if my heart still lives in the ocean or on top of mountains, far away from the hospital rooms I'm in now.

But whoso hath this world's good, and seeth his brother have need, and shutteth up his bowels of compassion from him, how dwelleth the love of God in him?

My little children, let us not love in word, neither in tongue; but in deed and in truth.

1 John 3:17-18

XV. BACK TO SCHOOL

When I decided to return to my academic studies, my journey took an unexpected turn when I was accepted into UC Berkeley. I couldn't shake the fact that, at over 40 with children, I didn't fit the typical student profile. Instead, I found my way to Stanford University, which welcomed me despite my less-than-stellar GRE scores.

I moved onto campus with my two children, determined to balance raising them with my rigorous coursework. Unlike other programs, Stanford's chemistry program did not require lab work, which allowed me to focus on my studies while managing my household.

Stanford was a child-friendly environment, but my time there was far from easy. I struggled initially, finding it challenging to adapt to academic culture. During my time there, I had a co-op student, someone who alternates between academic semesters with semesters spent working paid, full-time positions in their industry, working with me for two months. His initial enthusiasm for chemistry waned when his experiments repeatedly failed. I reassured him that failure was an integral part of the learning process and I reminded him why he was there.

Three years later, I saw him at a conference, and he shared that he had earned his master's degree in a year, crediting the perseverance he developed while working with me. I was honored to have played a part in his success.

Then shall the kingdom of heaven be likened unto ten virgins, which took their lamps, and went forth to meet the bridegroom.

And five of them were wise, and five were foolish.

They that were foolish took their lamps, and took no oil with them:

But the wise took oil in their vessels with their lamps.

While the bridegroom tarried, they all slumbered and slept.

And at midnight there was a cry made, Behold, the bridegroom cometh; go ye out to meet him.

Then all those virgins arose, and trimmed their lamps.

And the foolish said unto the wise, Give us of your oil; for our lamps are gone out.

But the wise answered, saying, Not so; lest there be not enough for us and you: but go ye rather to them that sell, and buy for yourselves.

And while they went to buy, the bridegroom came; and they that were ready went in with him to the marriage: and the door was shut.

Afterward came also the other virgins, saying, Lord, Lord, open to us.

But he answered and said, Verily I say unto you, I know you not.

Watch therefore, for ye know neither the day nor the hour wherein the Son of man cometh.

Matthew 24:1-13

XIII.

CAREER CALLS

For a nerd like me, spending all day with tech is a dream. I eventually "leveled up" as the kids say when I began working at HP labs. That was my big break. I was hell on wheels at it too. It only took us ten months of research and testing to develop a prototype that was nothing short of a miracle. Word spread throughout the community about what we had done, and the investment dollars came pouring in until we were heavily funded.

In the second year of my employment, the owner of the company hired another engineer. He was an unpleasant element in the office and would become a dark cloud the rested over the place during my last two years there. This man brought his best friends to come work with him and started them at salaries that were $50,000 higher than the rest of us. He would stand in the middle of the room, surrounded by his friends, and talk only to them, leaving the rest of us out of the conversation.

Finally, I went to the General Manager and told him that he was not the right person for our company. This new man was convinced that the rest of the staff was unnecessary. Worse, he wanted to restart the research that we had spent a year perfecting. The leaders of the company yielded to him, losing all the ground we had gained.

I vested my stock at HP after a few years and received a healthy sum. I thought I would buy a place in the British Virgin Islands since it was one of my favorite places on earth. I would sail every day and dance every night. At least, that was the fantasy.

Things at work grew more unbearable and I decided to leave the company.. That meant putting my dreams on hold a little while longer.

At this point, my older son Charles could see the difficulties I was having. He didn't want me to go back to work because he didn't want me to be around an office full of dangerous men. I was a good earner and could command a healthy salary. So, I returned to a company I had worked for in 1972. I worked there for a while before leaving under difficult circumstances. My supervisor hired an engineer who was quite green and didn't know much. He started as a trainee and was hired at a salary higher than mine, despite my degree, experience, and most importantly, results. When I found out, I couldn't believe it. I walked outside to get some air and steel my resolve. I came back inside and told me supervisor that it wasn't acceptable and I would be leaving.

I took another position with a new company. I was horrified to discover that this company was scrapping components they thought they couldn't use. I was shocked. I spent a lot of time figuring out a way to use them that I thought would please the leadership of the organization. It didn't. They were scrapping items as part of a larger scheme to cook the books. So, they had no interest in my ingenuity. I felt so disillusioned.

Shortly after, the president of my division invited one of my colleagues, who was also my friend, on a date. She called me after the date to tell me that he had drugged her, rendering her unconscious. He took her lifeless body someplace where he could sexually assault her. She regained consciousness just in time to see him removing her clothing. She was able to escape.

On top of it all, I discovered that the company was shipping products to people who didn't exist to make it appear that the company was doing more business than it was. They were swindling their investors out of thousands of dollars, buying products from their friends who headed the supply companies — products they trashed as soon as they received them. I had had enough. It was time to take a stand or move on.

I went into the office of the Vice-President, a very religious man, and told him how I felt. I said, "Listen, you can give me a very generous severance, and I will leave quietly."

Twenty years later, I returned to the company. I was desperate to work and felt I was a good fit. However, I learned that the turnover rate for my position was exceptionally high. Engineers in this company were being asked to do dishonest things. The company was perfectly happy to take advantage of them. I spoke to the leaders and insisted that they pay my team a salary that was commensurate with the work they were doing and on par with their counterparts in the industry. I got them to agree.

It was a great day when I got to tell my team that they would be making more money. One young man named Ricky had a particularly memorable reaction. I sat him down and told him that I had given him a raise of $20,000 per year. The look on his face was one of shock and disbelief. He could barely speak.

My boss was the vice president, a wily snake. He never graduated from college. I didn't discriminate. I had met plenty of smart people without degrees. But this man was unscrupulous and not very smart in creating such a contentious environment.

I created a plating shop for the company where we used gold, silver, copper, platinum, nickel using dangerous chemistries. Before me, the engineers had been so browbeaten, I had to admit that they weren't going to do a good job. Paying them more money was not enough to erase the years of abuse they had suffered, and I couldn't break them of the bad habits they formed to survive.

As a result, I ended up doing most of the work myself. I was the only thinker in the division and worked myself to death. It was a tough position to be in which further compromised my heart.

I did all the work to consolidate that plant, including bringing in a colleague to share the workload. My boss took that opportunity to fire me now that he had my counterpart at the other company to take my position.

Following that, I moved into consulting work. One of my first clients was a company Lockheed had started. They hired me to fix a product that was in production. I commuted 65 miles one-way to the location each day, evaluating the problem.

I went in with purity of heart but failed to put measures in place to protect myself. I developed a bolt for a cargo container that I received a patent for. If someone were to cut the bolt, it would send a signal to let the owner of the container know that it had been breached. We developed thousands of them. But the production of the bolt was inconsistent. We started cutting the bolts apart to investigate the problem. What I learned was that the steel was fracturing incorrectly. It was supposed to have a bit of pliability. I sent the failing bolts out for analysis. It turned out that the steel supplier was sending us the wrong steel and including toxic metals. The poor souls that worked in the plants in China and in the US were being exposed to cancer-causing materials.

The company offered to renegotiate my contract to fix the problem, but I agreed to continue under the agreement we had. That decision is a classic example of the ways I failed to take care of myself. I was too giving, too accommodating, and let far too much pass before taking a stand and finding my voice.

I wore myself out, working long hours to resolve the problem for them. Being the good Christian Scientist that I was (that I thought I needed to be), I pushed myself to the limit. Finally, my teacher told me that being a Christian Scientist was not synonymous with being a martyr. She encouraged me to get help.

Shortly after, the toll on my heart was too much and I started to notice that my health was declining. It was clear that I needed to make some hard choices and big changes.

I went into treatment and things got better. I got back into the job market and was offered a position at Hewlett Packard where I stayed for fourteen years until my health forced me into retirement.

What they say about a broken heart is true. I fear mine never recovered.

Let no man despise thy youth; but be thou an example of the believers, in word, in conversation, in charity, in spirit, in faith, in purity.
  1 Timothy 4:12

XIV. THE CHRONICLES OF TEENAGERS

As a single mother, I devoted myself to my children. My father outsourced some parenting to my mother. I could not do that. Firstly, I didn't believe that was the right tact to take as a parent. Secondly, there was no one to pass my responsibility to.

There was a 10-year period where I devoted myself to my children by not dating. I didn't want to be distracted by my own dating life when my children needed and deserved my full attention.

We had a lot of fun as a family. We made sure to enjoy ourselves. I loved to cook and we ate together every night. I invested lots of time and money in the boys, and sent them to Colorado for camp in the summer as much as I could.

Their enrichment and education were my job. . I got them involved in boating quite a bit. Other times, we visited museums. San Francisco's museums were geared toward children and made science, history and art interesting. I bought them skateboard clothing, took them skiing, and supported them as they played ice hockey. They were tall and skinny like me, already wearing tall men's clothes at 12 years old, with shoes sizes in the teens. It wasn't cheap to feed and clothe them. But we survived.

There are so many things you overcome in life that teach you what life is about. We talk a lot about those tough times often to the exclusion of the many fun memories we build.

I endeavored to teach my children to overcome limiting beliefs. The older I get, the more I am convinced that we underestimate the power of identity. Knowing who you are and teaching your children to know who they are is critical.

I taught my sons to use their intellect to interact with the world, not just their emotions. At the same time, I wanted them to be in touch with their emotions and unafraid to love. I wanted them to utilize their masculine and feminine sides. As I taught them, I learned as well.

My children had special challenges to keep at the forefront of their mind. As half-black, they would have to live differently in the world. As a single mother, and the mother of mixed race kids, we faced ridicule. People called them "oreo" or "Uncle Tom."

Once, my son came to me despondently and said, "Mom I keep getting stopped by the police." It was a conversation I hoped I would never have to have with my children, but I told both my sons to always stay polite and cooperate. I told them they would get shot if they ran from the police. It was a horrible thing to tell a child. I felt it was my job to tell them of the horrors that could occur in the hopes they'd have the smarts to prevent those outcomes. In today's world, it is far worse and they would certainly be under more persecution or hardship as darker-skinned men of color.

I raised my children consciously to avoid trouble. That said, I also taught them that if they were going to get in trouble, they should do it before they reached eighteen after which they would get records. Looking back, perhaps this wasn't the best parental advice. I wanted to instill in the two of them the importance of reputation while keeping the same open demeanor of my parents. Nonetheless, what I hadn't come to grips with then was the impossibility of keeping any of my parents' rearing methods in this chaotic environment.

Charles and Stephan listened well. They sowed their oats and made plenty of mischief — some I didn't learn about until years later. Of course, to keep them from their own embarrassment, I won't share any of that here. Perhaps they can spend time divulging in the ways they turned my hair grey in *their* memoirs.

I did not raise my kids to be Christian Scientists. I let them choose their own path. It was just my job to expose them to what I believed. It was up to them to explore other options and see what the world had to offer them. I believed the kids needed other perspectives so that they could make choices they would be able to commit to.

I would welcome their friends into our home. We gathered around our large dining room table that could easily seat ten. I fed them and simply listened to their stories. That is how I learned about what my kids were doing. I discovered that it was my older son, Charles who shut down a highway by setting off a smoke bomb under an underpass in Palo Alto.

Not to be outdone, Stephan and his friend, Justin, had gone onto Stanford campus when they were very young and came upon a motorized cart that was used to transport students who were injured in a game. Someone had left their keys in the cart. They seized the opportunity to go driving around. The Stanford campus, unlike the campuses in the east, were mostly fields, unmowed wild acres of treelined spaces. It made a wonderful playground for my children for two or three days after school. They hid the cart so that could retrieve it the next day. The wife of a professor discovered them and called the police, demanding that the city press charges against these two preteens. I showed up at the precinct to pick them up and the officers tried to give me two white kids. I smiled and pointed to the brown boys next to them. "Those are mine!" I'll never forget the look on the officer's face.

We made it through high school years without too much trouble. Charles went on to junior college, but Stephan had become a tad uncontrollable, During this phase, I sent him to Texas to live with his father. He was in the mode of destroying everything around him. He wrecked all of his good friendships. I thought, at that time, it was better to keep him with family than sending him off to boarding school as my parents had done with Micheal. I wanted to listen to my children while giving them some order, some sense of law and morality. When I saw that it was beyond my capabilities, I prayed until it was clear this was the best solution in keeping my son safe. A decision I think about often, but do not regret.

A friend, Nancy, helped me understand that Stephan was suffering from fear of abandonment. As he got close to people, he pushed them away. As he got successful at something, he destroyed it. He didn't want to be disappointed and avoided the good things in his life for fear they'd go away. I don't know if sending him away was the right choice. But it seemed to be the only choice.

Stephan was placed in a special school for children with disciplinary issues. I considered even placing him in a group home with trained professionals; however, the school did the trick, and he excelled and was quickly at the top of his class. I was relieved.

One afternoon at lunch, Stephan, close to graduation day, was sitting among the other classmates. The teacher warned the students to stay in the cafeteria. The punishment for leaving the room was that the offender would not graduate. Stephan defied her and walked right out of the cafeteria. He was forced to take an extra class to qualify for graduation because of his rebellion.

He continued to sabotage his life and some of his antics were dangerous. He also discovered a love of skateboarding. It was a perfect alternative for him. It held the danger that seemed to attract him, but it was also fun. And it put him in a community of other boys who were committed to skateboarding.

Charles was no less troubling. He got into a lot of fights when he was 15 in Palo Alto; kids chose him as a target despite his lack of provocation. People found him intimidating because he was tall and Black. Many young men lack judgment in their late teens and early twenties. Most get it back in their mid-twenties. Many others have confirmed that their boys made their worst decisions at that time of their lives.

Perhaps I was avoiding the truth about my children Or perhaps I just didn't know any better. I opt for the latter. I did the best I could, ensuring they at least had access to an education.

I needed help with my children. I needed someone to talk to. There was no one available to me. I turned to the church and got the brush off as if this was a personal thing I was struggling with. I found three families who, thankfully, were able to help me. Each family had children who were wonderful to me. They were babysitters for me as well as counselors when I needed it. They had come into my life just in time. They understood what I was going through.

Christian Science delineated people into two groups: learners and thinkers. The Christian Science text announced that this was the time of the thinkers. In my life, I needed someone to lean on. These families were my thinkers when I needed a break. I am so grateful for their love and openness.

Charles grew to be a kind and loving young man. He couldn't bear to see anyone harmed. It's one of the things I love most about Charles. He once saw a man, George, get knifed in a bar. He chased after the assailant, risking his own life. Then he tried to get the injured man to the hospital but the taxicabs wouldn't take him. He got the man to the hospital and saved his life.

George later lost his business during COVID. He was drowning financially. Charles, who didn't have much money to spare at the time, paid his rent and helped him in every way he could.

The sense of care and generosity of spirit runs deep in us both. It's a feeling of brotherhood with the entire planet. We feel a kind of unity with all people. Our hearts bleed for the downtrodden.

Stephan was a bright child. He could easily do well without even trying. He learned to pass so that he wouldn't have to work hard at the boring things (at least what he defined as boring) and apply himself in experiences he enjoyed.

Stephan got his master's degree from the University of San Francisco and worked in a school until an unfortunate accident with a classmate. Soon after he travelled to Nicaragua and Columbia to work and take some time to himself. Later, he taught at one of the universities in Columbia. He speaks Spanish fluently as if it is his native language. He might have stayed in Columbia but the drug cartels threatened him, educating the locals was cutting into their workforce and they threatened to kill him. Columbians didn't take prisoners at the time. They were not interested in ransom. Stephan only had two choices: return to the US or die. He was heartbroken that he had to leave. My father had experienced similar treatment when he was in Columbia.

Stephan has finally returned to the US and is doing quite well. He works with autistic children at one of the top schools in the company. They love him there. He is kind and incredibly intelligent, and Charles and I often say he was the brains of the family. I couldn't be more proud of his life and the path that got him here.

Now that I am in New York, I get to see them both frequently. I asked them recently if they thought they would have made it if I hadn't invested so much and so long. They both said no. I was glad to hear it even though I already knew the answer.

As for religion, the church was certainly a part of my children's upbringing. There are many ways to bring the value that religion and faith holds without demanding obedience to any organization outright. That was the approach I used with the two of them. Similar to my parents, however, I never sat either of them down to tell them what we believed. Certainly, Charles Sr. hadn't converted to Christian Science. The boys weren't living the same childhood I was and I knew early on this would affect their faith and entire outlook on the world. Their perceptions of good and evil would be morphed into something much different than my own.

Nonetheless, I was as open as they'd let me be. There was so much about Christian Science to love. While there are places where I diverge from the church, there are others where I am in wholehearted agreement. One of these places is in the Rule for Motives and Acts that I shared with my boys. This tenet is read the first Sunday of every month. It reads:

Neither animosity nor mere personal attachment should impel the motives or acts of the members of The Mother Church. In Science, divine Love alone governs man; and a Christian Scientist reflects the sweet amenities of Love, in rebuking sin, in true brotherliness, charitableness, and forgiveness. The members of this Church should daily watch and pray to be delivered from all evil, from prophesying, judging, condemning, counseling, influencing or being influenced erroneously.

~ Manual of The Mother Church

These small engravings of faith seemed to make an impact, which I see more now as they are adults and fathers themselves. I watched as my boys built relationships with women that are loving and respectful to them and their children. Stephan and Charles are outstanding fathers and husbands – unlike the men of my generation. They found the best partners and treat them with such kindness, I tear up thinking about it. I raised my boys to like women not just love them. I see their friendships with their partners and the rewards they reap through the happiness of their children. My beautiful grandchildren.

I taught my sons that sex was for making babies, but it was also for fun. I encouraged them to always use protection if they weren't planning to procreate. This is something I am proud of and relate to the free-thinking nature of my parents. That said, my mother would have opposed this. Most parents would have opposed this – in the 80's and now.

I told them when they were 15 or 16 to respect women. If they wanted to have sex, I encouraged them to protect themselves by using condoms. My parents never had these conversations with me. So, when I became sexually active, I was far too promiscuous and didn't always take proper precautions. My logic was to do the opposite to yield opposite results. I'm glad they listened. That said, I don't know if this success is because of my encouragement to explore or simply because of their nature to be good.

Being a mother has made me question this more than once. Perhaps we don't teach the nature of good or bad to our children, they simply are tender-hearted or not. In my case, I was proud of myself for doing so much on my own with the odds against me. However, in observation of their characters, my sons have taught me they had inherent gifts, gathered from I don't know where.

Today they are excellent fathers despite not being fully raised by their father. They were able to give what they never received. They are brilliant and cheerful men who have been invaluable in my life.

Today, Stephans' heart longs to travel. He has been saving his money in hopes of leaving the US. He wants to be in Costa Rica. I would miss him terribly, but I understand his longing. He would prefer Columbia, but the conditions there seem to be getting worse rather than better. Charles is a traveling man. His work takes him all over the world, giving talks. He's a world-class geographer and development specialist and speaks fluent Czech and Bahasa and is knowledge of other languages. His work in Caribbean, East Asia, and Africa is legendary. He fell in love with the people of the world who were kind to him.

His work history has been impressive. He has worked for NASA, the World Bank, CARICOM and the UN. He started a small cryptocurrency company to make blockchain technology and cryptocurrency available to everyone in the world, rich or poor, with a focus on the marginalized. People don't believe that he only started the company with the goal of helping others, rather than making money. In fact, he put more money into the company than he ever made.

The pride I feel for both my sons is insurmountable. There is no enjoyment I have felt greater than when listening to them talk, laugh, cry, or share moments with their children. My hope for them, long after I'm gone, is that they remember to love and find joy in their families. To never take it for granted. They've been my greatest accomplishments to date.

Children, obey your parents in the Lord: for this is right.
Honour thy father and mother; which is the first commandment with promise;
That it may be well with thee, and thou mayest live long on the earth.
Ephesians 6:1-3

XVI.
DISCRIMINATION'S INTERLUDE

I had a huge house built in San Francisco. It was a gorgeous 5-bedroom near the bay. A friend designed the house and built it. Everything in it was custom-designed for me.

The location was ideal for a people-person/loner like me. While I liked my times of solitude, I enjoyed having people around me. So, I spent my morning on the beach where I could quietly breathe in the waves while having others around me doing the same.

I sold my 5-bedroom and bought a slightly smaller 3-bedroom, 2-bath home with a lovely garden and a million dollar view. I was proud of my accomplishment and the new life I'd built. I planned to work until I was 65 and then retire happy and healthy. But fate had other plans.

I worked for a man who hated my guts but needed someone with my skills. He fired me when I was 62 and at a vulnerable time in my life. It was my plan to work past 65. But I decided that I would retire rather than continuing to face that kind of abuse. It was the right decision because I ended up with heart failure and couldn't do very much anymore.

There is no real benefit from self-pity. But I wish that the time I had set aside to care for myself in retirement could have been used to replenish the money I spent on my children's education, supporting them through graduate school.

I developed an infection in my lungs that made it hard to work. I had to step down from my position and attend to my health. Suddenly, with a big, beautiful new home, I had no more money coming in.

In those days of financial struggle, money was tight. I was burning through everything I had saved and watched helplessly as my bank balance grew more and more anemic. I lived on ramen noodles since each pack was less than a dollar.

My failing health crippled my ability to earn an income. The fear of poverty did my heart no favors. Sadly, I didn't know how sick I was. I almost died before discovering that I was developing a heart problem.

I had a good team of doctors whose treatment pulled me back from the brink. I started to feel healthy and strong again. But as soon as my mind turned toward returning to work, the heart problem returned. Once again, I was fighting for my health.

I would have to find a way to live and support myself. I had this beautiful home that my savings and investments afforded me. Perhaps… just perhaps the house could make me money.

I started investigating the Airbnb market and found that it offered two benefits I craved: money and meeting people. And boy did I ever meet people. I had guests check-in from locations all over the world. I got to meet them and hear their stories, learning about their travel. But some guests touched my heart more than others.

Two gay Black men once stayed at my home. We became fast friends. They shared that they had been poorly treated and even denied a stay from other places. They constantly had to worry when they traveled that they wouldn't receive a warm reception due to both racism and hatred of their sexual orientation. Both men expressed their appreciation for how nicely I treated them.

What they didn't know what how much I related to their struggle. I was acutely aware of times when I was on the receiving end of unfair treatment where my gender had more to do with how I was treated than my skills and contributions to my company.

One of those times happened when I talked to my supervisor at the semi-conductor plant where I had worked early in my career. I had an idea about how to streamline the manufacturing process and essentially eliminate one entire step in the chain. The implications of the idea were huge as it would save the company a massive amount of money and increase productivity.

My boss waved my idea away at the time. I wasn't offended that he didn't think it was an idea worth sharing, though I couldn't understand why he didn't jump on it immediately.

Shortly after, I was scheduled to go on vacation. That meant I would miss a couple of high-level meetings where processes and other important business would be discussed. I learned that, in my absence, he floated the idea I had shared with him! Worse, he took complete credit for it as if it was his brainchild!

I sat for a long time pondering what to do after I found out about the betrayal. It was not common to challenge one's boss in those days, especially as one of the only women in the company. Many men thought I should consider myself "lucky" to have the job at all. Besides, there was a price to pay for taking a stand. I risked losing access, promotions, opportunities, etc. But this was a slight too big to ignore. So, although I knew there would be a penalty, I confronted him and asked why he would do such a thing.

His reply?

"Your turn will come," he said, suggesting that the same larceny that sprang from his dark heart was lurking in mine, and I would use any opportunity to do to another what he had done to me.

I remember thinking, I am nothing like you! I would never do what you've done!

I walked away from that meeting despondent, wondering if his behavior was due to his power, his gender, sheer evil, or some combination of the three.

Thankfully, I had worked very closely with an engineer who happened to be a woman. She and I had the pleasure of doing some research together that resulted in a patent which she and I owned jointly. Our professional relationship grew into a close personal friendship. I even attended her exquisite wedding at a botanical garden.

I felt she was the right person — perhaps the only person — I could talk to about this. I contacted her, told her the story, and asked, "Margaret, do they treat you the way they treat me?"

"Oh no!" she exclaimed. "They treat me much worse. With me, they feel they have a right."

As a woman in a male-dominated field, I had to deal with less-than-optimal working conditions. The men around me would take any opportunity that presented itself to marginalize me, including speaking in a foreign language so that I wouldn't understand the conversation.

Once, in a gathering of colleagues, several of the men spoke in Mandarin, leaving me out of the conversation completely since I didn't speak Mandarin at all. I watched their faces, listened to them laughing together, noticed when the speaker said something that made them all nod. A pit of despair churned in my stomach at their behavior. So many people championed the cause of women or minorities. But, when it was time to put up or shut up, their mouths slammed closed tighter than a bank vault.

It wasn't always terrible. At the very least, I was sometimes invited to special events. I will never forget eating dinner at a Chinese executive's home and consuming the best hot pot meal I'd tasted. The meal was exquisite as was the décor. It was a lovely experience. But it didn't make up for the losses in the workplace I had suffered throughout my career. And it didn't get me access to the table.

Some organizations aren't healthy. They might be large. They might be profitable. But none of that equates to health and wholeness. When a current of emotional immaturity, racism, sexism, nepotism, or any other cultural ill runs through a company, the organization is rotting from the inside out.

We have seen giants fall all around us — companies that seemed too big to fail ultimately failed because there was no truth at the heart of their existence. In essence, these companies had no beating heart. Like a chicken that continues to run after its head is chopped off, these companies look like the picture of health before they suddenly atrophy into oblivion.

San Francisco was supposed to be different. The people there prided themselves on having the right message about sexuality, race, gender equality, etc. But I saw so much injustice occurring all over California, it broke my heart to watch it.

Still, running the Airbnb was a blessing. It met my needs and supported me quite well. But even that was threatened by my health. I started to feel weaker day by day. It was hard to clean. Once I tried to change the linens and could hardly pull the sheets around the mattress. A voice that must have been the voice of God spoke clearly in my mind, saying, "You can't do this anymore."

I told Charles what happened.

He smiled and said, "Yeah, Mom. It's time to let it go. Why not move to New York so you can live closer to me?"

I had great friends in San Francisco. I found it easier to make friends as I got older than I did when I was middle-aged. But I wanted to be closer to Charles. We had discussed it, but the prospect of moving was daunting. I had accumulated so much: ceramics, dishes, art, furniture, and a fine collection of cookbooks. Some of the furniture pieces were more like works of art. I had a whole host of tools and appliances that I felt were priceless. Those I sold to a neighbor. Most everything else I gave away. People were so thrilled and appreciative.

I gave as much as I could to the Salvation Army thinking that some poor person would come in and be able to buy something of great quality for a low price. Besides, the Salvation Army employed people other organizations and companies rejected. Ex-convicts applied to work there when others wouldn't consider their applications.

We emptied the house in the space of two weeks by boxing what I wanted to take and selling or giving away the rest. There were miraculous days. We would have a large item that we wanted to go to a new owner. Sure enough, someone would come looking for exactly what we had put up for sale.

It would be easy to give away things I did not want. But much of what I owned were things I wanted and saved more. Much of what I bought was the result of hours of research to ensure I was getting something of great quality. It was tough to let go of some things like my book series.

I purposely tied my money up in different financial instruments because I knew that if I had liquid cash, I would spend it on my kids. I had a nice nest egg in savings and used the sale of the house to purchase a new place. Where most people put down 20 percent and finance 80, I did the opposite. I either put down 80 percent or paid cash in full. I didn't want to be in debt or leave a financial mess for children to sort out.

*F*or so is the will of God, that with well doing ye may put to silence the ignorance of foolish men:

As free, and not using your liberty for a cloke of maliciousness, but as the servants of God.

Honour all men. Love the brotherhood. Fear God. Honour the king.

Peter 2:16

XVII.

COAST TO COAST

Charles and I packed up my house, giving away so much of what I had accumulated over decades to people in need. When it was all said and done, I had given away enough to easily justify a $20,000 tax deduction. I moved to New York and rented an apartment not far from Charles on Roosevelt Island. There was no way for me to know how I would adjust to life in New York, so I decided to give it a year! The last time I moved to NYC was during college, when I moved into a top-floor brownstone apartment in Needle Park (Sherman Square). Miles Davis lived in the neighborhood and I often saw him with exotic women.

Now living in an apartment with a window that overlooked the East River was one of the most enchanting experiences of my life. From the first day I moved in, I knew that this view would delight me. Each moment, from dawn to dusk, the river told its story, serving as the backdrop for a beautiful dance of nature and urban life.

Every morning, the sun rose over the horizon, glowing its golden rays across the water, making it shimmer like liquid gold. The light nudged me to life each morning, sending me in search of my morning coffee before watching the Manhattan and Brooklyn skylines come alive. This was a side of New York far different from the one that birthed and nurtured me in my childhood.

Skyscrapers reflected the morning light all over the city in a dazzling display of colors. Boats and ferries glided along the river, leaving white lines behind as if they were painting the water's surface. The iconic Queensborough bridge stretched across the river, adding its timeless beauty to the scene.

The city sparkled at night with its twinkling lights along the glittering skyline as New York slowed down long enough to catch a second wind and start again in time for night life. This was a far cry from the sleepy farms and fields I came to know when I last lived here. I like it. I revel in it's angst. I had grown and evolved. Therefore, it was understandable that I needed the pace of this version of New York to quicken my steps. I knew it would once the COVID-19 lockdowns had passed. Until then, I could only watch the cautious and the brave from my perch high above the river.

The buildings and bridges came alive anew at night, showcasing their architectural beauty against a black sky. The river was calmer after dark, almost serene as its surface grew mirror-like, reflecting the cityscape back to anyone who took time to look.

As the years have passed, and I've continued to dwell in this exhilarating city, I continue to be awe struck by its energy. The city, much like the world, has changed drastically over the years. That hasn't stopped me from finding small ways to breathe in the city life around me.

On clear days, I could see the constant activity on the water. Despite the COVID pandemic and heavy restrictions, the faithful runners, bikers, and walkers made their way to their usual places, even if six feet apart. The land flanking the river hosted them, offering parks and greenery as well as places to rest along the riverbanks.

Weather played its part with misty rains dancing on the river's surface or thick fogs shrouding the city in a hazy veil. No wonder so many people loved New York. I was falling in love as well. The East River was there with me throughout the difficult days of COVID, reminding me that some things never change. Through tranquility and chaos, light and darkness, joy and pain, it was my silent companion, there to greet me each morning.

I was alone during COVID. No one could visit me and I couldn't go to be with them. Technology was my only connection to others during those days of solitude. But I was OK with it all. While I loved being with others, I was always at peace about being by myself. My only fear was that the health issues that had been compounding would reach a tipping point and land me in an overcrowded hospital and exposed to infection.

I needed to be especially careful about what I did and where I went, knowing that I couldn't go out without taking great care. That reality sometimes brought on a sense of loneliness that was uncharacteristic for someone like me. Our family had been close and enjoyed getting together from time to time. And I had a reputation for being the one who accepted everyone and embraced who they were without question. People knew they could come to me and find a shoulder to lean on — acceptance without judgement. But no one came because they could not come.

It wasn't long before I was missing them and they were missing me. As soon as restrictions were eased, I got as active as I physically could, participating in various events. But my health issues remained relentless. I seemed to only get sicker and sicker.

After a few months, I made the decision to stay in New York and sell my house in San Francisco. I also chose to give up renting and buy. This time, I bought a coop in the same building where Charles lived, leaving the rental apartment behind. Breaking the lease was an expensive proposition because, during a pandemic, it was difficult for the management company to re-rent the unit. I was socked with a $30,000 fee to get out of there. A week after I moved, New York was on lockdown and no one was accepting new residents. You couldn't budge if you lived anywhere in New York. I had just made it and breathed a sigh of relief even though the financial impact of both moves was tremendous.

The move was difficult. My new place, though just as beautiful as the one I left, required extensive cleaning. The prior owners had left plenty of chores for me to do to bring it up to the par, including evicting the roaches that had taken up residence there.

Charles poured his efforts into remodeling the place and did a stellar job. He even positioned the kitchen counters higher than normal, which I loved because of my height.

Once again, I was up to my ears in dozens and dozens of boxes stacked from wall to wall inside. Walking from one room to the other was akin to navigating a maze. Though I had given so much away, there was still a plethora of "stuff" that had moved from one coast to the other. Once the boxes were mostly emptied, I got busy with life. After the unpacking was complete and the socializing began, it was time to tackle whatever was going on in my body. I needed to get to the bottom of my physical health concerns, submitting to extensive testing to see where my doctors and I needed to focus to get me well again. Mercifully, I was able to avoid any hospital visits for two years by working hard on myself and with my medical team.

What does it truly mean to grow old? Sure, there is the older and wiser bit we talk about. Yet, there are some unlovely things about being old that I had to learn and accept.

I learned what I didn't like about ageing, the isolation, the uncertainty around health, and the lack of mobility. I also learned a lot about society's views about the elderly and how expectations change as you age. I saw stark differences between the men and women in my community. I watched as men aged quietly, content to park in front of the television or behind the pages of a newspaper, only socializing when escorting their wives here and there. The women, on the other hand, were former lawyers, judges, politicians, etc. and other professionals who didn't see retirement as a time to slow down. They stayed active in their senior centers and social groups.

The pandemic was a stressful time for everyone. But for those over 60, the warning that seniors were at a significantly higher risk was disquieting. We saw the images of the dead piling up in makeshift morgues in NYC and around the world, wondering if and when COVID would strike us or someone we loved.

People used all sorts of methods to deal with the fear and the grief they faced. For me, turning to my religious beliefs in a new way was the answer. I devoted more time to praying for the world, particularly the operation of truth in our dialogue. The line between what was true and what wasn't had seemed to be blurring. But there was something about the pandemic that redrew those lines more starkly. People facing their own mortality tend to also consider their own morality. As a people, we had to face who we really were, what we believed, what we stood for and against, and what truly mattered in our lives.

I did my best to engage in self-reflection and realized that we would never go back to what we were as a nation and a world. There was no back to return to. It was all gone, and a new reality would need to be crafted in order to replace it. It was a new Orwellian Age.

I wrote some responses to articles published in the New York Times. Many of them were accepted. I spoke about the political landscape and how alarming things were.

With all that was happening, though, the greatest lesson might be the one of humility. Others and I had to face the fragility of life as well as its brevity. We had to acknowledge that so much of what we thought mattered, didn't. It was time to re-prioritize and look at our world through a new lens politically, spiritually, socially, and personally.

*Trust in the Lord with all your heart
and lean not on your own understanding;
In all your ways submit to him,
and he will make your paths straight.
Proverbs 3:5-6*

XVIII.
INTROSPECTION

The pandemic taught us a kind of introspection that most living people had never known was possible. It forced us to slow down dramatically and confront aspects of our lives we often overlooked in the relentless hustle and bustle of everyday existence. With lockdowns and social distancing measures forcing us back inside our homes, either alone with our thoughts or confined with the people we were closest to, many people found themselves spending unprecedented amounts of time thinking about their lives with startling clarity and depth.

While there was indeed great devastation, profound sickness, and heartbreaking loss touching nearly every family and community, the enforced solitude provided a unique and unexpected opportunity for deep reflection. Of course, I am no stranger to such a mass infestation of grief although this time, I have the experience to navigate with faith.

The isolation allowed us to evaluate ourselves with the honesty that our busy lives had previously made impossible. We were compelled to take a hard, unflinching look at our priorities, our core values, and the relationships we claimed to hold most dear. The pandemic's numerous challenges pushed us to confront many of the difficult questions we had skillfully avoided for so long, forcing us into an uncomfortable but necessary reckoning with ourselves.

We finally got honest with ourselves in ways we had been avoiding for years, perhaps decades. We assessed our mental and emotional well-being with a thoroughness that felt both frightening and liberating.

Some of us were genuinely surprised to discover hidden reserves of strength and resilience we didn't even know existed within us, while simultaneously uncovering areas of our character and psyche that desperately needed attention and growth.

Perhaps most challenging of all, we had to become comfortable with profound uncertainty, imagine that! In a world where knowledge has become power and answers to virtually every conceivable question seem only as far away as our fingertips, we suddenly found ourselves in a situation where we didn't know anything for certain. The questions mounted relentlessly while the answers remained frustratingly elusive. Medical experts contradicted each other, government policies changed daily, and predictions proved unreliable. In this unprecedented fog of unknowing, all we could do was learn to let ourselves find and enjoy the inner peace that comes from acceptance, appreciate the unexpected quiet that had settled over the world around us, and rediscover the simple joys that truly sustain us through life's most difficult passages.

While the often contradictory and sometimes hypocritical behavior of public figures made them easy targets for criticism and scorn, I realized the pandemic represented a precious opportunity to examine my own life with the blinders completely removed. This was my chance to evaluate some of the choices I had made throughout my years with brutal honesty. The questions I posed to myself were searching and uncomfortable: Was I as kind as I could have been to the people in my life? Was I as loving and generous with my affection and support as I liked to believe? Was I continuing to grow as a person, or had I allowed myself to atrophy in some fundamental way, becoming stagnant and self-satisfied?

No period of my life felt off-limits for this intensive introspection. I reached back into my earliest childhood years, asking hard questions about who I was during those formative times and what had motivated me to do the things I had done. I wanted to look at that younger version of myself with compassion but also with clear eyes, asking her if any unresolved issues were lingering in her psyche that I could finally address now, as an adult with the wisdom and perspective that comes with age and experience.

One particularly vivid memory immediately sprang to mind, unbidden but insistent in its demand for attention and resolution.

As a young girl, probably no more than twelve or thirteen, I had fallen asleep one winter night praying earnestly that the weather forecast calling for good snow would prove accurate. My prayers were answered completely, I woke up to discover freshly fallen snow blanketing everything outside my bedroom window. Such a scene was always an irresistible invitation to play, and I knew instinctively that all the other children throughout our neighborhood would be racing to find their warmest boots, heaviest coats, and waterproof gloves, eager to take advantage of this winter gift I managed to bestow.

I genuinely enjoyed spending time with most of the kids in our close-knit neighborhood. We were a diverse group of personalities and ages, but we generally got along well and created elaborate games and adventures together. However, there was one boy I actively disliked and, if I'm being completely honest, feared. He had developed the disturbing habit of chasing me during our group activities, and when he managed to catch me, he would touch me in ways that were unmistakably sexual and that I despised. These encounters left me feeling confused, violated, and powerless. I couldn't have been older than thirteen at the time.

When the neighborhood children gathered eagerly to play on that particular snowy day, we immediately set about the serious business of building elaborate snow forts and rolling perfectly round snowballs in preparation for what we anticipated would be an epic winter battle. The air was filled with excited chatter, strategic planning, and the kind of joyful energy that only comes from unexpected freedom and perfect weather conditions.

That's when I spotted the boy who had been tormenting me, and something dark and calculating stirred within me. Without really thinking about the consequences or the moral implications of what I was contemplating, I reached down and picked up a rock, not a pebble, but a substantial stone that would cause real pain. With deliberate intent, I carefully inserted it into the center of the snowball I held in my mittened hand, packing the snow tightly around it to create what was essentially a weapon disguised as innocent play equipment.

I reserved that dangerous snowball specifically for this boy, and when the opportunity presented itself, I hurled it at him with all the force and accuracy I could muster. The satisfaction I felt when it struck him was immediate, but short-lived, quickly replaced by a complex mixture of guilt, shame, and disturbing recognition of my own capacity for cruelty.

This may sound overdramatic, but it still made me ponder long enough that this single act of calculated violence stayed with me for years afterward. It was something I had never forgotten, being deliberately and coldly cruel to another human being, regardless of how he had treated me. The memory would surface at unexpected moments, bringing with it a bit of shame.

During this pandemic period of intensive self-examination, I finally felt ready to confront this long-buried incident directly and honestly. I recognized that while the boy's behavior toward me had been inappropriate and hurtful, my response was not something to be proud of. That's not who I am.

After years of contemplation, I understand I am not at fault for how he acted, I am only responsible for my own actions. This lesson has stayed with me in adulthood during many difficult interactions in my professional and personal life. While his actions were wrong, they didn't define my entire character or determine my worth as a human being. By extending this forgiveness to my younger self and him , I freed myself from the haunting power this memory had held over me for so many years.

This process of confronting and resolving old wounds was far from a mere academic or intellectual exercise. What could be more powerful, more transformative, than confronting yourself: past, present, and future, with complete honesty and ask the hardest possible questions? This kind of deep self-examination allows you to integrate all aspects of yourself fully and authentically, without the destructive burden of shame, paralyzing fear, unresolved trauma, or the poisonous weight of unforgiveness toward yourself or others.

What could be more important or life-changing than this kind of radical self-acceptance and integration? The pandemic, for all its devastating losses and challenges, had given me this unexpected gift: the time, space, and motivation to finally make peace with parts of myself I had been avoiding for far too long.

For though I would desire to glory, I shall not be a fool; for I will say the truth: but now I forbear, lest any man should think of me above that which he seeth me to be, or that he heareth of me.

And lest I should be exalted above measure through the abundance of the revelations, there was given to me a thorn in the flesh, the messenger of Satan to buffet me, lest I should be exalted above measure.

2 Corinthians 12:6-7

XIX.
WHERE I AM

I woke up one day to discover that I was in the hospital. At least, that is where I thought I was. It was hard to tell. The people around me were speaking a different language — or so it seemed. I thought I had been kidnapped and transported to a different country. Wires snaked around my body, IV's poked into my arms, and I was muzzled with some sort of apparatus I couldn't get off.

Finally, someone explained that I had ended up in the hospital after experiencing a cardiac event. It was a terrifying way to regain consciousness.

I found most of the nurses who cared for me to be good and kind and wonderful. But there were certain types of nurses who were awful — so much so that it's almost unbelievable that they are in a profession to serve the sick and/or elderly. These types of nurses draw other like-minded individuals with darkened souls to themselves until they have formed a gang of cold-hearted cruel practitioners who don't belong in a hospital setting caring for the sick.

One example occurred when I discovered that the nurses caring for me had composed a song about me, ridiculing my condition and mocking my need for care. Together, her coven crafted nicknames to describe me and other patients as well as the guests who came to visit us. They gave Charles the moniker "Obama" because he was clearly of mixed race, and they called my son, "Cain," an especially nasty name. The tormenting extended to the minors who came to the hospital as well as they devised cruel names for each of them. And I... I was called the "Engineer."

I was blessed with exceptional hearing as a child and would astonish the audiologist each year when he came to test the children in my school. Each year, the audiologist would try to test the limits of my hearing playing sounds softer than any other child could hear. He finally resorted to pretending to play sounds to see if he could trip me up. He couldn't. I knew when there was a sound and when there wasn't.

I used my bionic hearing to listen to the conversations taking place outside my room, though I think anyone who was half-trying could have heard their awful words and the witchy cackles that followed their cruel jokes. I transcribed their conversations and forwarded them to Charles.

When it was time to leave the hospital, I received my discharge papers and packed to leave. I was more than ready to escape what I felt was a kind of torture chamber. There was a bandage that had been wrapped around my arm at some point during my stay. The nurse wanted me to hang around and give her a chance to take it off, but I couldn't get out of there fast enough.

When I got home, the bandage ached so badly, I started working on unraveling it from my arm. When I pulled the last of it off, I saw that there was nothing beneath it. There was no wound, no device, no entry point for a catheter, nothing. Why had this bandage been wrapped so tightly around my arm, except to hurt me?

As bad as the hospital stay was, my post-hospital recovery time was even worse. I had gone into the hospital fairly strong and left it barely able to move. Everything was difficult: walking, standing, bathing, feeding myself, etc. How could this have happened to me seemingly overnight — living independently at home one day and stuck with IVs flowing some foreign substance into my body while wearing a breathing apparatus the next day?

I've never been a physical fitness buff. But I've always been active and loved sports. Though I wasn't a fan of organized sports, I gravitated to activities that tested my physicality, which has resulted in maintaining a healthy weight. However, after that hospital stay, I made a new commitment to physical fitness and strength training so that I would not be at the mercy of nurses like that anytime soon in my future. I needed so much help and care in the early days after leaving the hospital for the most basic functions. But I kept attempting to do things that seemed outside of my physical abilities so that I would push my muscles to grow and adapt. I was able to build my physical strength the best I could and far beyond where it was. I still tire easily and need longer recovery times than I used to. But I could only imagine where I would be if I had not put in the work to improve.

I learned a great deal from this experience. As much as I want to believe there is good in the world, I had to accept that there is an abundance of hurting people who hurt other people as a means to anesthetize their pain. I learned the value of good health. And I learned that I was blessed to be surrounded by people who cared for me when I couldn't care for myself.

I was also making new friends in my community. I had found a haven of "old bitties" who were seriously accomplished women in their youth. They leaned on walkers and canes. But their minds were as sharp as they were twenty years ago. Some had been entrepreneurs and CEOS; others were politicians; and some had worked as doctors and lawyers. Somehow, they escaped traditional domesticity and found their place in society like me. No, there aren't many of us. But there are enough.

I love getting to know the women in my community. When you scratch their surface, you find that they are fascinating people who have had incredibly rich and meaningful lives.

As we have therefore opportunity, let us do good unto all men, especially unto them who are of the household of faith.
Galatians 6:10

XX.
PATH OF FAITH

Life can be tough and rough. That's a ridiculously reductive statement but it's true. All people need a reservoir of joy that they cultivate throughout their lifetimes and draw from when their happiness and contentment run dry. That truth has remained with me whether I was in a hospital bed or standing on the summit of a majestic mountaintop.

I have allowed life to interest me and take me from one height to another. When I hit lows, I took my lumps, evaluated my failures, and extracted whatever lessons I could. In truth, I reject the idea of failure altogether. There is no failure — just data. The data tells you the results of your actions — nothing more. It doesn't pass judgment. It doesn't scold. It doesn't blame. It simply gives you the information you need moving forward.

That is why I say failure is a great teacher. Failure exposes the chinks in your armor or, better yet, the gaps in your knowledge. It lets you know where to focus your efforts at strengthening and rebuilding.

I have been blessed to watch my family walk the path of faith, trusting that any and every failure was only a gateway to the next big opportunity in their lives.

My grandmother had a hard life, never knowing her mother, who died in childbirth and being orphaned at the age of twelve. It was a sad development in a life that was destined for greatness. She turned her difficulty into a quest for her destiny. As a result, the woman who was "on the shelf" became a stellar mother and wife.

My father had a hard time in parenting his boys. But he grew as a man as his sons matured. He learned to appreciate both Micheal and Ralph in time.

My mother and father experienced hard times when they failed to get a mortgage for their dream house. The mortgage lender came over to our house to tell them that their loan was denied. My mother burst into tears at the news. It was one of the few times I saw my mother cry. She was inconsolable as their hopes and dreams for their ideal house went up in smoke. My father looked desolate, feeling as if he had disappointed my mother and let the family down. Moments later, their eyes met, and they burst into laughter as if to say, "Look at us crying over this when we have such a great life."

It was one of the greatest lessons I learned by watching them be who they were. They took life in stride, expressed real emotions, and then opted for gratitude over despair.

What I have seen and experienced as a life-long practitioner of my faith is that it's my responsibility to nurture to storehouse the joy in my own heart. I have done this to the best of my ability. I have had incredible adventures to balance the trials life brings. I have learned to approach life from the standpoint of the all-consuming power of Love. That is where I find the very structure of my mentality and, in it, the force that feeds my joy.

My mother talked to me about prayer and commandments. She never believed Jesus was God, but she valued the 11th commandment: Do unto others as you would have the do unto you. She learned the only cure for fear is love.

The prophet and leader Moses was told, "The place where on you stand is holy ground." The same is true for us. Even in the worst situations, in the face of defeats, and certainly in times of joy and successes, we are at all times on holy ground. Therefore, it is natural that we should daily reap the rewards of life in the presence of God.

Sometimes, the reward is simply the strength to carry on in the face of despair just as we do in happy times. Life is never all roses and sunshine. We must deal with the weeds and the rain. But even in those times, the goodness and sacredness of life never leaves us. We continue to support each other in prayer as Truth, Life and Love are invoked and we move toward a kinder, fairer, and more loving society.

The Sermon on the Mount set the standard for the effectiveness of prayer as demonstrated for our benefit by Christ Jesus. In one message, Christ Jesus was able to put life in proper perspective for all who heard him.

My heart aches for the state of humanity and all of the ills we face. The issues that are closest to my heart are concerns I continue to pray for and work toward:

- There is a great need for good design in housing and building shelters that are gracious and easy to inhabit.
- We must learn personal care for the human body - how to be clean and comfortable.
- We need quality food that is tasty and fresh.
- We must find ways to transform our society to accommodate those in need and put to work those who are able to contribute.
- We must be an accepting society that embraces all people with love.

None of us can claim perfection. We have all sinned if we define sin as missing the mark. Just as an archer pulls back on her bow and aims for a target, each of us endeavor to be the best we can and do the best we can.

In that noble pursuit of righteousness, we stumble and fall. We want to always hit the bullseye, doing everything in lockstep with our values. But when we miss the mark, we have only responsibility; that is, to try again.

In truth, each time we miss the mark, it adds value to the times when we hit it. It is rewarding to finally hit the mark, knowing that each attempt brings us closer to the vision of the person we want to be.

XXI.

Wherefore, as by one man sin entered into the world, and death by sin; and so death passed upon all men, for that all have sinned: For until the law sin was in the world: but sin is not imputed when there is no law.
Romans 5:12-13

THE NEXT GENERATION

Life, at its core, is about love. It is the love of family, the warmth of romantic love, the camaraderie of friends, and the passion for the ideas that illuminate our path. My journey has been colored by these different loves, each shaping me and guiding my steps. Among these, the love for my boys stands as one of the greatest joys and triumphs of my life.

As a mother, I have watched my sons grow from curious, wide-eyed children into remarkable men. The journey wasn't always easy, but it was always worth it. Every scraped knee, every late-night conversation, every triumph and setback—they all forged a beautiful bond between us. Today, I see them not just as my sons but as fathers themselves. Watching them nurture their own children, I am filled with a sense of pride and fulfillment. Their kindness, strength, and integrity are reflected in my grandchildren, who carry forward the legacy of love and values that I cherished and instilled.

My love for Christian Science has been another cornerstone of my life. It provided me with a spiritual framework that has guided me through life's challenges and triumphs. The teachings of Christian Science taught me resilience, compassion, and the importance of seeing the good in every situation. This faith has been a beacon, lighting my path and shaping my worldview. It has given me the strength to face adversities with grace and to celebrate the blessings with gratitude.

Engineering, too, has been a passion and a calling. As a woman in a field traditionally dominated by men, I found my place and made a career that not only provided for my family but also allowed me to contribute to a world that constantly evolves and innovates. The discipline, problem-solving, and creativity inherent in engineering have always resonated with me. Each project, each challenge, each breakthrough, added a layer to my professional and personal growth.

The choices we make as women are pivotal. They can lead us to a life of fulfillment or one of stagnation. I chose to pursue the path that made my heart sing. It was a path that required courage and a belief in myself. And through it all, love was the constant. The love for my family, my work, my faith, and my ideals kept me moving forward, even when the road was steep and the obstacles seemed insurmountable.

Today, as I look at my sons and their children, I am overwhelmed with joy. The sight of them brings tears to my eyes—not of sorrow, but of profound happiness. In them, I see the continuation of a journey, the perpetuation of love and values that will carry forward into future generations. It is a legacy that I am proud of, one that reaffirms the importance of love in all its forms.

Life has taught me that love is the most powerful force we possess. It is the foundation upon which we build our lives, the force that drives us to be better, to strive for more, and to cherish the moments we have. It is in love that we find our true purpose and our greatest joy. And it is through love that we leave a lasting impact on the world and those we hold dear.

CONCLUSION

Therefore, my brothers and sisters, you whom I love and long for, my joy and crown, stand firm in the Lord in this way, dear friends!

I plead with Euodia and I plead with Syntyche to be of the same mind in the Lord. Yes, and I ask you, my true companion, help these women since they have contended at my side in the cause of the gospel, along with Clement and the rest of my co-workers, whose names are in the book of life.

Rejoice in the Lord always. I will say it again: Rejoice!

Let your gentleness be evident to all. The Lord is near. Do not be anxious about anything, but in every situation, by prayer and petition, with thanksgiving, present your requests to God. And the peace of God, which transcends all understanding, will guard your hearts and your minds in Christ Jesus.

Finally, brothers and sisters, whatever is true, whatever is noble, whatever is right, whatever is pure, whatever is lovely, whatever is admirable—if anything is excellent or praiseworthy—think about such things. Whatever you have learned or received or heard from me, or seen in me—put it into practice. And the God of peace will be with you.

Thanks for Their Gifts

I rejoiced greatly in the Lord that at last you renewed your concern for me. Indeed, you were concerned, but you had no opportunity to show it. I am not saying this because I am in need, for I have learned to be content whatever the circumstances. I know what it is to be in need, and I know what it is to have plenty. I have learned the secret of being content in any and every situation, whether well fed or hungry, whether living in plenty or in want. I can do all this through him who gives me strength.

Yet it was good of you to share in my troubles. Moreover, as you Philippians know, in the early days of your acquaintance with the gospel, when I set out from Macedonia, not one church shared with me in the matter of giving and receiving, except you only; for even when I was in Thessalonica, you sent me aid more than once when I was in need. Not that I desire your gifts; what I desire is that more be credited to your account. I have received full payment and have more than enough. I am amply supplied, now that I have received from Epaphroditus the gifts you sent. They are a fragrant offering, an acceptable sacrifice, pleasing to God. And my God will meet all your needs according to the riches of his glory in Christ Jesus.

To our God and Father be glory for ever and ever. Amen.

Final Greetings

Greet all God's people in Christ Jesus. The brothers and sisters who are with me send greetings. All God's people here send you greetings, especially those who belong to Caesar's household.

The grace of the Lord Jesus Christ be with your spirit. Amen.

Philippians 4

I often chuckle at the suggestion that young people are paying into government programs to support seniors. While I understand the math (and the optics), the truth of the matter is that there is a kind of reciprocity happening between the generations. When I think of all my generation suffering that has resulted in a better life for people today, a meager social security check or a Medicare health plan hardly compensates for all that seniors today have offered the world.

Furthermore, there is still a treasure trove of untapped resources my generation possesses that could be shared with those who have come after us. But younger generations don't ask and older generations don't offer. Instead, we see each other as an impediment to our goals when we should be close allies.

I cannot speak a word of wisdom to the future generations without speaking a word to my own. To people my age, I encourage a new commitment to stay active, involved, and relevant. The voices of the senior generation are necessary. That may be as simple as writing replies to articles or as intricate as getting involved in community activities. We cannot fade into the background or our tongues to lie silent in our mouths. We are a part of the intricate stew that is American life; therefore, we must participate.

For those who are younger than me, I would offer this wisdom: the best people to surround yourself with are those who rejoice at others' happiness. They wear a smile even if not on their faces. They ease the way for others and want to see good things happen for everyone around them. They hold a special kind of joy about life even in the midst of their trials. They embrace life with optimism.

Conversely, those who harbor jealousy, envy, and strife destroy everything they touch. They are far from wisdom, happiness, or love even though it may be right at their fingertips. They can't perceive it, and will never allow those around them to enjoy dancing in the light.

Furthermore, I encourage younger generations to embrace faith. Whatever form your faith takes, practice it with sincere dedication. Grow in your knowledge of your faith, embrace the laws of spiritual healing, and study faith with discipline and wonder.

Mary Baker Eddy, the woman who founded the Christian Science movement, often hosted classes for students who wanted to grow in their faith. In one such class, she asked her students a profound question:

"What is the most important thing of all?"

The overwhelming answer was "Love. Love is everything."

The students explained that it is because of love that we live and move and have our being. It was love that created us and it will be love that is with us until the very end of this life and at the beginning of the next. Love sustains us in everything we are and all that we do. And, for Christian Scientists, love represents the power of God.

"Wrong," Eddy replied. "The most important thing of all is wisdom."

The students were shocked and horrified at her answer. She explained that, without wisdom, love is never acknowledged or accessed.

We require wisdom to both give and receive love. It is wisdom that leads us to the truth of God's love for us. Love and truth come together under the banner of wisdom.

I tend to agree. When you reach my age, if you haven't given up or sold out, you learn the value of wisdom to keep you connected to God and others. Wisdom teaches you to live your life rather than letting it all go by. Wisdom urges you to fight for what you believe in rather than thinking it is someone else's responsibility to do the hard work.

Wisdom is a time-tested attribute. It comes from doing the work and sacrificing in your life to be a person of value and worth. Just like anything, only a commitment to go the distance results in success. We live in an age where people like to dip their toes in the waters of life. But wisdom teaches that you must be all in on life to experience the richness it has to offer.

I've been fortunate to find several oceans in life to jump into. I've been full throttle about the things and people and causes that matter most to me, and that is what has made my life worth living. These are the things that I have given myself to. And I've been having a blast!

I have been complimented on my cheerful disposition. People often say they find me upbeat, pleasant, humorous, and positive. They are right. I wish I could say that it's because everything in life has gone my way. But now that you have read my story, you know that isn't true. The truth is that I am always smiling through extreme pain and discomfort. By this time in life, most people have a whole host of ailments coming along for the ride.

I suffer from a heart problem that makes it difficult for me to breathe. My balance is poor and I use a walker to get around. My cardiologist says it is a good sign that I haven't been in the hospital for the past two years. I count that as one of God's many blessings and keep moving forward in my life. I know that it was and is God's love for me and my love for God that allows me each day that I live.

So why cheerfulness? I learned long ago the power of a positive attitude to heal. Adopting a positive attitude in spite of everything is a powerful approach to life that can lead to more growth and happiness. In a world filled with uncertainties, challenges, and setbacks, maintaining a positive mindset can be difficult. But I have learned how essential your attitude can be when working to overcome obstacles. If you want to have a good life, it often starts with your thought of life. This is where faith becomes indispensable. Trusting in God's plan is an essential foundation to my faith and it helps me navigate through health challenges or whatever else life throws my way.

Our attitude influences how we see the world around us and how we respond to situations, people, and events in our lives. A positive attitude gives us the power to approach our lives with optimism, hope, and a belief that, even though it's tough sometimes, things will ultimately be OK. It enables us to see opportunities where others see obstacles and to persevere where others see impossibilities.

One strategy I have always used to cultivate and maintain my positive attitude is practicing gratitude. It's easy to complain about what isn't happening or the illnesses we suffer or all that isn't right in the world. But gratitude suggests a different approach. By focusing on the things we are thankful for, we shift our attention away from negativity and towards appreciation. This can be as simple as stopping each day to think of three things we are grateful for. It only takes a moment, but the benefits are exponential. Cultivating gratitude helps us develop a more positive outlook on life and helps us maintain feelings of contentment and fulfillment.

It can also help to reframe negative thoughts. As I mentioned earlier, instead of complaining about my heart condition, I choose instead to be grateful that I haven't needed to be hospitalized in two years. So often we wallow in our negative thoughts. But, instead of dwelling on setbacks or failures, we always have the option to choose to see them as opportunities for growth and learning. If nothing else, we can always give thanks for the gifts we have: the gift of family, friendship, love, the beauty of nature, and just another day to be alive.

By reframing our perspective, we can turn challenges into stepping stones towards success. This requires us always be in the mode of practicing shifting our negative thoughts to more positive and empowering ones.

No, life isn't all rainbows and sunshine. Having a positive attitude does not mean ignoring or denying real emotions. We all have negative emotions sometimes. We can especially feel them when we are dealing with illnesses. That's never fun. It's natural for us to sometimes experience sadness, frustration, or even fear at times. It's also healthy to acknowledge these emotions and confess that sometimes we must cry. We all must cry sometimes. However, maintaining a positive attitude means that we don't stay in a perpetual state of sorrow. We dry our eyes and turn our focus to solutions, searching for the silver lining in every situation. I have learned to view tragedy, discomfort, and all of life's ills in the light of gratitude.

If I were asked the secret to a good life, my answer would have to be that there is immense joy in pursuing your dreams and following your vision. It's critical for everyone to know who they are and what they are meant to do in the world. Some of us are fortunate to learn that very early on in life. But, for others, it may take some time and experimentation to find that place of purpose we seek.

None of us knows what tomorrow brings. At my age, that is more a reality than ever. But I know that each new day brings new opportunities to laugh and love. I recommend doing both as much as you can.

The nature of family teaches many of life's greatest lessons. Through family, we learn the art of unconditional love. Family teaches us the value of connection — lifelong commitments to others who love us in return. Family teaches us the skill of working together toward common goals and standing beside each other through thick and thin.

As a woman, my life could have gone in many different directions. I was fortunate to have a mother and grandmother who showed me the best there was about woman hood. They lived the lessons they wanted me to learn. I learned that the choices women make will determine their contribution to the world. A woman's path to acceptance is not determined by society, the political climate, or her husband. She can be a force for good in the world if she chooses. At this point in my life, I am still a learner. I am useful to the world in ways I never thought I could.

Do good in the world. I mean that literally. Though we pray and believe for good things to happen, we must devote our lives to something that will change lives. I received a visit from a former Sunday School student who is giving her life to stopping human trafficking. Others are serving in the UN. Some are working on a local level to give aid to those who need it most.

There is nothing more nourishing for the soul and more impactful in the world than giving of yourself to others.

The following is a collection of recipes, memories of Kristin, and excerpts provided by family and friends.

Allison Kephart
20 August 2024

There is no adequate way to summarize twenty-nine years of connection. Twenty-nine years of being known, and now fourteen years of mentorship, friendship, and admiration. There is an irreplaceable depth of understanding when someone has known you since birth, witnessing and nurturing the formation of your worldview, listening to your dreams and fears, and encouraging your wildest aspirations. At almost fifty years my senior, Kristin's advice, intelligence, and kindness have been a guiding light my whole life.

How do I find the words to adequately describe how much I loved my friend? I wish I could tell her today's news, I wish I could bring others to meet her too. I wish.

I could ask her how to move with purpose, how to know you're doing the right thing, and how to continually believe in change.

Kris knew me from before there was a me to know. She held me when I was mere days old, watching me grow up from diapers and dresses to graduation gowns and business suits.

A core early interaction that has stuck with me was when I was about twelve and just starting to observe the world deeply for the first time. Kristin and I both found ourselves over for tea at the home of a member of our church congregation. A cozy Sunday afternoon with great company. I made a round of the room, offering tea and cookies to the people who had known me my whole life. That day, the adults took an interest in my thoughts and weighed my responses into consideration for their reflections. This was new, exciting, and bonding for Kris and me. Speaking with her on a deeper, philosophical level, we addressed how the world and it's many issues influenced my ambitions. I walked away that afternoon with my burgeoning interest in global affairs fed and stimulated, my perspectives treated as legitimate and worthy of interest.

When I was sixteen, Kris became my Sunday school teacher. While my other teachers directed me in intensive analysis or a strict understanding of Christian Science, Kris and I directly addressed real-life news, social issues, and global affairs. For the first time, I walked between faith and global issues that spoke to my heart. Kris gave me the space to think deeply about life, providing new tools and perspectives to analyze its many layers. And, even more, my place within them.

I recall most of all being excited for Sunday School because I knew we would analyze the happenings of the week, or some new crisis of electoral freedom or human rights deserving of dedicated, heartfelt attention.

I don't remember when I realized our relationship was special and so very precious. Perhaps it blossomed first unseen, but with a deep sense of knowing, two kindred spirits, twirling instinctively.

When I graduated high school and left her fold, we both knew it was not the end of our connection. Over the years we've kept in touch via emails and bi-annual phone calls. Through my undergraduate degree I called her 'mentor'. Through my master's and into my professional life I called her my friend. Every so often we would schedule an extended phone call and, regardless of our starting point - what's new, how's work, how are classes- we would inevitably wind up discussing how to best approach our responsibility to the world, and how to act in times of crisis and pressure to navigate decisions when no "right" path is evident.

With every interaction, I walked away grounded, more deeply set in empathy and love for others and this world. Even when I left our conversations with no clear answer as to what decision I should make next, her words quieted my heart, pacified my doubts, and steeled me towards the road ahead.

Kris demonstrated what it means to have unwavering faith in an uncertain world. Kris' faith in the world, despite its difficulties, was unshakeable. When those seeking her guidance, as many often did, came to an impasse of not knowing where to dedicate our energies next in life, Kris spoke with a deep and quiet conviction that our pathways would unfold before us. This knowledge radiated with an irreplicable warmth and energy, ensconcing me too in this sense of knowing. Often, her complete confidence that I was on my intended path and conviction that my next best step would reveal itself in its own time resolved the unease in my heart.

Kris demonstrated how to move with both dignity and humility, diligence and patience. How to gracefully accept notions of difficulty or strife while maintaining a conviction that they can and will be addressed as they should, in time.

With Kris, I could be honest about my feelings about the world- my concerns for the future, fears that I am inadequately prepared for whatever purpose lies ahead, that I am too impatient or headstrong in a world too far broken. At each juncture of concern and milestone (undergraduate and master's graduation, starting work and its tensions, moving abroad a second time), she listened patiently, thoughtfully, and with gentle wisdom and fondness to the concerns of youth. Kris never made my feelings seem small or insignificant; often, she would meet my internal conflicts with examples from her life where sentiments folded into my own. Despite decades more of life experience (and what a life it was!!), she always approached our conversations with warmth and a joy for listening, treating our councils as a meeting point where our hearts and minds could collaborate. Her friendship was a gift I treasured every time we spoke, and every moment in between.

Few people in the world understand my heart better than Kris. This, I've come to realize, is what it feels like to truly be known.

Perhaps that is why I feel the weight of all the thoughts I want to share with her, all the crossroads of life where I crave her guidance, so acutely. It seems like every other day that I note something- a lesson, a feeling, a new fact about the world, that I want to tell my closest mentor and confidant. I want to consult with her- is the world a beautiful place, or are some fractures too deep for mending? How do we dedicate our love most purposefully when the world hurts in so many ways? Where do I go from here, how do I know where I'm meant to be? I wish I could ask her how to know when to let go and when to stand your ground, if there is something she could share that could help me believe in the meaning of what we're doing and all we hope to achieve.

When my heart grows conflicted and overwhelmed by the challenges of the world, when an internal turmoil triggers a deep-set sense of unease about my place or path, there is a hollowness where our phone call should be. I have, in this time of absence, grown acutely aware of what it means to be thoroughly understood as a person. I have so many things I want to tell her. So many things I want to ask her, to consult, to talk through, to understand. I wasn't done. I treasured every conversation we had. Every phone call, every text, every holiday greeting- and it still wasn't enough. Kris' friendship, mentorship, guidance, and counsel has been one of the greatest gifts I have ever received.

Sometimes, it's hard to move forward without her critical insights. As a young woman at the start of my career, I occasionally feel lost in direction at life's intersections. Although the truth is that I have been guided so resolutely for so long that, although I crave our detailed councils on the world and my future. Kris's wisdom still resonates, safe in my heart. I know that I can lean into her conviction that I, our country, and the absolute truth of what is just and right, will find our way.

Kris often referenced Mary Baker Eddy's words, "The time for thinkers has come." Kris was one of the deepest thinkers I have ever met and one of the smartest people I will ever know. I am blessed to have been her student, to have grown up under her wing, to have navigated a world full of complexity and contradiction with her love and keen insight as a guide. Kris was one of my dearest friends. We shared a heart in many ways. No passage of time will take away the lessons she has taught me or lessen the love of our friendship. It is all I can do to approach my friends and mentees with equal attentiveness, a love that stretches so deep that they feel seen and held, to approach their concerns with patience and gentleness and hold them in my thoughts as lovingly as I was held. It is all I can do, in writing these words, to hope to impart some small impression of the incredible impact Kris has had on my life, and the continuity of her enduring lessons.

It is truly one of the greatest blessings to have been her student, mentee, and friend.

CORNBREAD

Ingredients:

- 1 Cup Yellow Cornmeal
- 1 Cup White Flour (or 2 Cups Corn Flour)
- 1/3 Cup White Cane Sugar
- ½ Tsp. Salt
- 4 Tsp. Baking Powder
- 1 Egg (slightly beaten)
- ¼ Cup of Softened Unsalted Butter
- 1 ½ Cup Whole Milk
- 3 Generous Tbs. Sour Cream
- 1 Tsp. Freshly Grated Nutmeg

Instructions:

1. Preheat oven to 325 degrees Fahrenheit
2. In a clean mixing bowl, sift dry ingredients together
3. Add Milk, Sour Cream, Nutmeg, Egg, and Butter
4. Stir well with a wooden spoon
5. Pour contents of the mixing bowl into buttered iron corn-muffin pans
6. Place in oven for 20 minutes, or until lightly browned on top.
7. Serve and butter while hot.

Sweet and Sour Green Beans

Ingredients:

- 1lbd Green Beans
- 4 Slices Bacon
- 1 Small Finely Chopped Onion
- ¾ Cup Cooking Water from Beans Stock
- ¼ Vinegar
- 1 Tsp. Honey

Instructions:

1. Fill a medium pot with water and bring to a boil
2. Prepare a bowl of ice water, set aside
3. Place Green Beans in boiling water, sit for 8 minutes
4. While Green Beans cook, chop Bacon and place in a frying pan
5. Once Bacon is brown, add onion to pan and sauté until translucent. Bring heat to low flame
6. Strain Green Beans from the pot, and immediately place them into an ice bath
7. Add vinegar and honey to pan, stir until brown
8. Add Green Beans

SALAD DRESSING

Ingredients:

- - 1 Cup Canola Oil (canola preferred so it won't solidify in the fridge)
  - 1/3 Cup Balsamic Vinegar
  - 3-4 Cloves of Pressed Garlic
  - 1 Generous Tsp. of Poupon mustard

Instructions:

1. In a medium size salad bowl, mix Garlic and Poupon Mustard until a creamy consistency
2. Add Oil and Balsamic Vinegar to the salad bowl and mix until all ingredients blend together
3. Add your choice of lettuce and toss until all leaves are well-coated. Serve immediately

Warm Potato Salad

Ingredients:

- 2 lbs Potatoes (of your choice)
- 1/2 Cup Olive Oil
- 3-4 Tbsp Red Wine Vinegar
- 2 Tbsp Lemon Juice
- 1 Tsp. Dried Oregano
- 1 Tsp. Salt
- 1/2 Tsp. Freshly Ground Pepper
- 3/4 lb Mushrooms (of your choice)
- 4 Ounces Snow Peas
- 1/4 lb Cooked Ham, Pork, Beef
- 1 Red Pepper
- 1 Rib Celery
- 3 Tbsp Parsley
- 1 Leafy Lettuce Stock

(add sliced 3 hard-boiled eggs if preferred)

Instructions:

1. Fill a pot with water and bring to a boil
2. Prepare a bowl of ice water, set aside
3. Dice the Potatoes, Celery and Mushroom, set Mushrooms and Celery aside
4. Add Potatoes and Snow Peas to the boiling pot
5. Cut the red pepper into strips, set aside
6. After a few minutes, remove Snow Peas from pot and plunge into the ice bath
7. Cut Snow peas into strips, set aside

8. Cut all cooked meat into strips
9. In a large bowl, mix all seasonings, Vinegar, Juice and Oil until blended
10. Once soft, drain Potatoes from the boiling pot, set aside
11. Add Meat, Red Pepper, Mushrooms, and Celery to the mixing bowl, toss until all veggies are coated in oil and seasonings
12. Add Potatoes to the mixing bowl, toss gently so Potatoes are well-coated without smushing them

*If adding Eggs:
1. Bring a separate pot of water to a boil
2. Add 3 whole eggs to the pot and let rest for 7 minutes
3. Prepare an ice bath in a separate bowl
4. Remove eggs from the boiling pot and immediately plunge them in an ice bath, let rest for 2 minutes
5. Peel the shell from each egg
6. Dice egg and add to mixing bowl after step 11 in previous instructions

APRICOT ICE CREAM PUDDING

Ingredients:

- 1 package (3 ¼ oz.) Vanilla Tapioca Pudding
- 1 Tsp. Ground Cinnamon
- 4 fresh California Apricots
- ½ pint Vanilla Ice Cream

Instructions:

1. Prepare Tapioca Pudding according to the package instructions
2. When Tapioca is removed from heat, stir in Cinnamon
3. Pour contents into serving dishes and chill until set (about 15 minutes)

To serve,

1. Cut Apricots into 4 sections and arrange on Tapioca
2. Cut Ice Cream into cubes and drop in the center of Tapioca and Apricots

Serve at once. Makes 4 servings.

Easy Apricot Fritters

Ingredients:

- 4 Fresh Apricot Halves
- 1 Cup sifted All-Purpose Flour
- 1 Tbsp Melted Unsalted Butter
- 2 Eggs
- 1/8 Tsp Salt
- 2 Tsp Lemon Juice

Instructions:

1. Beat eggs until very light
2. Add all other ingredients plus just enough cold water to make a batter like heavy cream
3. Dust apricot halves with flour and dip in batter
4. Fry in deep cooking oil or shortening
5. Drain and dust with powdered sugar
6. Top with a tart

FRESH APRICOT RIPPLE ICE CREAM

Ingredients:

- 1 ½ Cups pureed or mashed fresh Apricots
- 1 Tbsp fresh Lemon Juice
- ¾ Cup White Cane Sugar
- 1 Quart Vanilla Ice Cream
- ½ Cup Heavy Cream
- ¼ Tsp. Almond Extract

Instructions:

1. Mix Apricot puree with Lemon Juice and Sugar
2. Chill for 30 minutes
3. Soften Ice Cream slightly
4. Whip Cream and add Almond Extract
5. Mix puree, Ice Cream and Whipped Cream quickly but not thoroughly – just enough for a ripple effect
6. Freeze until firm
7. Serve with additional pureed fresh Apricots for a tangy topping

Serves 6-8.

BUTTERMILK PIE

From Katinka Schilling Brigham with modification from Kris Brigham

I double the ingredients - then I cut the sugar by about 1/4 Cup, maybe a little less, as the taste needs to be great AND SOME SUGAR IS A GOOD THING.

-Kris

Ingredients:

- 1 Cup White Cane Sugar (if doubling, use 1 1/2 Cups, minimum)
- 3 Tbsp All-Purpose Flour
- 3 Egg Yolks
- 2 Cups Buttermilk
- 2 Tbsp Melted Unsalted Butter

Instructions:

1. Heat oven to 350 degrees Fahrenheit
2. Grease you baking dish with Oil or Butter - *I butter a souffle pan or other large baking dish with high sides*
3. In a small bowl, sift Flour before adding Buttermilk, Butter, Sugar, and Yolks, mix WELL
4. In a separate bowl, whip Egg Whites to stiff but not dry
5. Fold Egg Whites into the Buttermilk mixture
6. Pour into pastry shell
7. Pinch of salt
8. Blend using whisk until smooth taking your time making sure that lumps do not form

9. bake at 350 deg for 45 minutes - be sure it's done!
    I always double the recipe but use 6 eggs and 5tbsp flour, 7tbsp of butter. It will make a lot and you can adjust it to your liking for dryness of buttermilk "sauce" on bottom.

This was a special treat which I (Kris) loved as a child as did my sons Charles and Stephan. Also, buttermilk is good for you and low calorie!

Plum Duff – Mom's Grandma (Katinka Brigham)

Ingredients:

- 2 Eggs beaten
- 1/2 Cup White Cane Sugar
- 1 Cup Brown Sugar
- Cup Mashed cooked Plums
- 1 Cup flour
- 1/2 Tsp. salt
- 1 Cup of Whole Milk

Instructions:

1. Butter a 1 litre/2 pint pudding basin
2. Mix the Flour and Sugar in a large bowl
3. Add the Plums
4. Add the eggs and mix well
5. Gradually add milk, stirring constantly, until the mixture will drop from the spoon when pulled from the bowl (dropping consistency)
6. Place the plum mixture into the pudding basin and cover with greaseproof paper or a pudding cloth
7. Secure the paper or cloth with kitchen string
8. Using a pan with a lid large enough to comfortably contain the pudding basin, half-fill the pan with boiling water. Add the pudding basin and cover with the lid. Steam the pudding for three hours. Replenish the water level if necessary.

9. Remove the basin from the pan and allow to cool slightly.
10. For the sauce, whisk the egg for five minutes until light and foaming
11. Add the sugar, butter and whisk well
12. To serve, spoon out the plum pudding onto plates and spoon the sauce alongside

Brigham Family Nutty Fruitcake

Ingredients:

- 1 Cup Brigham Black Walnuts
- 1 Cup Brigham Pecans
- 1 Cup Brigham Figs
- 1 Cup Almonds
- 1 Cup Dates

1 Cup Raisins

- 2 Fresh Apples
- 1 Cup English Walnuts
- 1 Cup Whole Wheat Flour
- 2 Eggs
- 1 Cup Unsalted Butter
- 2 Tbsp Molasses
- 2 Tbsp Honey
- 2 Cloves
- 2 Tbsp Cinnamon
- 2 Tbsp Allspice
- 1 Cup Apple Juice

Instructions:

1. Lightly grease and line a 10-inch springform pan with parchment paper
2. In a large saucepan melt the butter over medium heat and add the raisins, dates, brown sugar, molasses, spices and juice
3. Bring to a gentle boil and slowly simmer for 10 minutes

4. Remove from heat and allow to cool for 30-45 minutes
5. When cool stir in the beaten eggs
6. Sift together, flour, baking powder, baking soda
7. Add the ground nuts to the sifted flour mixture and fold through the boiled mixture
8. Fold in apples, dates, figs and all of the nuts
9. Pour into prepared baking pan. You can decorate the top with additional nuts, cherries etc., if you like
10. Bake at 300 degrees F for up to 2 hours or longer depending upon the size of your pan
11. At this point you can poke small holes in the top and bottom of the cake with a fork and pour on 4 ounces of dark rum or your favorite whiskey, half on the top, wait ten minutes, then flip it over and pour the remaining half on the bottom
12. Soak several layers of cheesecloth in additional rum if you like and wrap completely around the cake, then cover with several layers of plastic wrap and store in a COOL place
13. When serving, you can add a layer of marzipan or if you have decorated the top with fruit and nuts, brush with a simple glaze of equal parts water and sugar boiled together for about 10-15 minutes

Apricot Crumble

Ingredients:

- 2 Cups sliced fresh Apricots
- 1 Cup Graham Cracker Crumbs
- 1 Tbsp Lemon Juice
- 1/2 Cup Brown Sugar
- 2 Tblsp Melted Unsalted Butter
- Light Cream

Instructions:

1. Combine Brown Sugar, Graham Cracker Crumbs, Melted Butter and Lemon Juice
2. Blend gently with sliced Apricots
3. Spread in a shallow buttered baking dish
4. Bake at 350 degrees for 25 minutes
5. Serve with light cream

Serves 6.

Bye, for now.
    Not forever.
  -Kris

www.ingramcontent.com/pod-product-compliance
Lightning Source LLC
Chambersburg PA
CBHW052308300426
44110CB00035B/2173